DARK HORSES
JUMPS GUIDE 2018-2019

DARK HORSES
JUMPS GUIDE 2018-2019

MARTEN JULIAN

Raceform

Published in 2018 by Raceform Ltd
27 Kingfisher Court, Hambridge Road, Newbury RG14 5SJ

Copyright © Marten Julian 2018

The right of Marten Julian to be identified as the author of this work has been asserted by him in accordance with the Copyright, Designs and Patents Act 1988.

All rights reserved. No part of this publication may be reproduced, stored in a retrieval system, or transmitted in any form or by any means, electronic, mechanical, photocopying, recording, or otherwise, without the prior written permission of the publishers.

A catalogue record for this book is available from the British Library.

ISBN 978-1-910497-70-8

Designed by Neil Wadsworth

Printed and bound by Page Bros, Norwich

CONTENTS

INTRODUCTION	7
THE PREMIER LIST	9
THE DARK HORSES	25
THE DARK HANDICAPPERS	55
THE POINT-TO-POINT GRADUATES	69
TAKING A LOOK BACK	99
THE TEN TO FOLLOW	107
THE 2019 CHAMPION HURDLE PREVIEW	123
THE 2019 CHELTENHAM GOLD CUP PREVIEW	137
INDEX	159

Keep in touch

If you want to keep in touch with Marten's thoughts on a regular basis then read his **free-to-view** journal at:

www.martenjulian.com

or ring him on

0906 150 1555

Selections given in first minute.

Calls charged at £1.50 a minute at all times & your telecom provider will add their own Access Charge. Please contact your provider for their charges.

Telephone & Text Service

A non-premium rate version of this line is available. Please call the office if you'd like to join or order online. The line is an 03 number which is the same as calling a landline and included in a mobile phone package. Marten sends a text message direct each day. Prices available online.

Follow Marten
@martenjulian

Tel: 01539 741 007   Email: rebecca@martenjulian.com   www.martenjulian.com

INTRODUCTION

Thank you for buying this 2018-19 edition of the *Dark Horses Jumps Guide*. I hope that you find it a useful source of reference and enjoyment throughout the course of the season.

As always I am hopeful that the horses selected for the Premier List will yield a profit. It is my belief that they possess the specific attributes to warrant our interest.

The Dark Horses section includes horses from a variety of backgrounds, notably recruits from France and the point-to-point field.

The Dark Handicappers section identifies a handful of horses that appear to be starting their campaigns from favourable marks.

My assistant Jodie Standing is especially excited about the quality of recruits from the Irish point-to-point field this year. We are pleased to be publishing for the first time *Point-To-Point Recruits*, packed with her in-depth analysis of almost 80 horses. The pick of her selections appear in this book.

Jodie has also written a retrospective piece on last year's recruits and also given us a handful of horses to follow under Rules.

I hope that you enjoy reading my previews of the Gold Cup and Champion Hurdle. As is so often the case these days, plans are very uncertain this far in advance, but I hope to have covered most of the eventualities.

As always I am indebted to my daughter Rebecca, Jodie Standing, Julian Brown, Neil Wadsworth, Steve Dixon and Paul Day. I am especially grateful to Ian Greensill for his painstaking work at the editing and proofreading stage.

If you wish to keep updated with my news and information then refer to my website www.martenjulian.com.

My weekly appraisals and assessments on the progress of the Premier List qualifiers can be monitored through the *Weekend Card*.

You can hear my views on a daily basis on 0906 150 1555, where any selections are given within the first minute of the message (calls charged at £1.50 a minute at all times). If you would like an alternative means of acquiring this information without paying premium rate charges, then please contact Rebecca (01539 741007) for details of the Telephone & Text Service.

Finally I would like to wish you all the very best of good fortune in the coming months.

Bye for now.

Marten

THE PREMIER LIST

The following horses have been selected for this section in the hope and expectation they will reward support through the course of the season.

ACEY MILAN (4YR BAY GELDING)

TRAINER:	**Anthony Honeyball**
PEDIGREE:	**Milan – Strong Wishes (Strong Gale)**
FORM (BUMPER):	**21114 -**
RATING:	**None**
TRIP:	**2m +**

One of the best bumper performers of his generation, displaying both stamina and speed in both success and defeat.

Built on the promise of his runner-up spot at Exeter on October when overcoming obvious signs of inexperience to beat Grand Sancy by nine lengths in an extended 1m 7f "Junior" Open NH Flat race restricted to three-year-olds at Wincanton in December.

Appeared next at Cheltenham on New Year's Day in a 1m 6f Listed race for four-year-olds, making all and quickening in the straight in the heavy ground to win comfortably by three and three-quarter lengths from Malinas Jack.

Took on his seniors next time out in an extended 2m Listed race at Newbury, travelling well and then leading two furlongs out to win from a good field which included Good Boy Bobby, who ended the season the winner of three of his four starts, dual winner Brewin'Upastorm and previous Newbury winner Morning Vicar.

Acey Milan – heading for the top

His final run came in the Weatherbys Champion Bumper at the Cheltenham Festival, where he was just one of four four-year-olds in the field. Up there with the pace as usual, he seemed to be going as well as anything on the descent for home before coming wide up the nearside rail and being outpaced for a few yards, then plugging on very gamely to hold fourth in a duel to the line with eventual fifth Blackbow.

Has always displayed a good attitude but was particularly tenacious in defeat at Cheltenham, fighting bravely all the way to the line.

Brother to Lord Wishes, a winner up to 2m 6f, and a three-parts brother to William's Wishes and Beggar's Wishes, both winners at around 2m 4f.

A horse of exceptional potential, blessed with those vital attributes of speed, stamina and courage. Everything you could wish for in a potential top-notcher and is in very capable hands.

Hugely exciting and must be on the shortlist for the Supreme Novices' Hurdle in March.

AYE AYE CHARLIE (6YR BAY GELDING)

TRAINER:	Fergal O'Brien
PEDIGREE:	Midnight Legend – Trial Trip (Le Moss)
FORM (HURDLE):	3F4304 -
RATING (HURDLE):	145
TRIP:	2m 4f +

Consistent staying novice last season, highly tried on occasions but never disgraced.

Shaped well in bumpers, winning at Southwell in January 2017, and made a promising start to hurdling last autumn when third of 10 to On The Blind Side in a 2m 4f maiden hurdle at Aintree.

Came up against the winner again the following month in a Grade 2 contest at Cheltenham, behind but not yet asked for an effort when falling three hurdles from home.

Returned to Cheltenham for an extended 2m 4f Listed contest in heavy ground in January, not disgraced plugging on at the finish into fourth, before again doing his best work in the later stages behind Santini over the same trip in testing conditions.

Raised again in class for the Ballymore Novices' Hurdle at the Festival and ran better than his finishing position of seventh suggests, keeping on gamely at the finish, although beaten 24 lengths by Samcro.

Fergal O'Brien – has charge of Aye Aye Charlie

Ran his best race to date a month later in a Grade 1 contest at Aintree, looking outpaced a mile from home before finishing with a flourish into fourth and staying on strongly after the line.

Half-brother to stable companion Chase The Spud, winner of the extended 4m 1f Midlands Grand National, from the family of Pensham, winner of 44 point-to-points.

Apparently likely to stay over hurdles for the time being. Crying out for three miles and could prove top class over that trip. Has already performed creditably with the best of his generation and now has to show he can win at that level.

Will relish a strong pace with the emphasis on stamina.

CARIBERT (5YR BAY GELDING)

TRAINER:	**Harry Fry**
PEDIGREE:	**Ballingarry – Cardamine (Garde Royale)**
FORM (BUMPER):	**121 -**
RATING:	**None**
TRIP:	**2m 4f**

Long-term chasing prospect but can make his mark over hurdles having impressed in fair bumper company last season.

Heavily backed and made all to beat subsequent winners Hideaway Vic and The Russian Doyen on his racecourse debut at Wincanton in November, keeping on strongly and finding a change of gear in the final furlong despite a slightly high head carriage.

Possibly came up against a smart one when failing to concede 7lb to subsequent winner Time To Move On next time at Exeter before returning to winning form when making all to beat Hotter Than Hell, a mare rated with black type potential, conceding her 18lb in a valuable Goffs UK Sales Bumper at Newbury in March.

Half-brother to four French winners at around two and a half miles. Rated a potential top-notcher for chasing by his trainer but can make an impression over hurdles before then.

May require two and a half miles or a stiff track over two miles to show his best but a lovely prospect for the future with both stamina and a turn of foot.

free blogs & newsletters **follow** the king of dark horses
www.martenjulian.com @martenjulian

DOLOS (5YR BAY GELDING)

TRAINER:	**Paul Nicholls**
PEDIGREE:	Kapgarde – Redowa (Trempolino)
FORM (CHASE):	13202 -
RATING (CHASE):	152
TRIP:	2m +

A decent hurdler, successful twice and rated 135, but better over fences.

Jumped with great confidence when beating Sternrubin, rated 143, on his chase debut over 2m 3f at Ascot in November but distant last of three back there just under a month later, possibly failing to stay.

Ran much better next time at Sandown, back over 2m and in his first handicap chase, losing momentum with a mistake at the second last but battling on bravely to finish a half-length second to the vastly more experienced Gino Trail.

Early morning at Ditcheat

Put up a remarkable display next time out in the Grand Annual Handicap Chase in March, dropping well behind after a couple of sloppy jumps, before picking up from the home turn to power up the hill and finish a never-nearer seventh, beaten just under 20 lengths (147).

Unlucky to come up against a rejuvenated Theinval on his final start at Ayr in April, leading two fences from home and headed by the winner halfway up the run-in (147).

A consistent, tough, lightly raced sort with youth on his side. Looks the ideal type for a top handicap chase, probably around a stiff track or over a trip beyond two miles.

KAPCORSE (5YR BROWN GELDING)

TRAINER:	**Paul Nicholls**
PEDIGREE:	**Kapgarde – Angesse (Indian River)**
FORM (CHASE):	**1 -**
RATING (CHASE):	**128**
TRIP:	**2m 4f +**

Very interesting lightly raced prospect with the potential to land a decent handicap chase or two this season.

Shaped in most encouraging fashion on his sole start in France, leading before falling away, only to stay on again in a 2m 2f three-year-old hurdle at Auteuil in October 2016.

Ran a fair race on his UK debut in a 2m 1f novices' hurdle at Exeter, finishing sixth of 17 having been up with the pace in the early stages. Not given a hard time the following month at Newbury before finishing down the field from a mark of 118 in his first handicap at Sandown in February.

Turned up in April for an extended 2m 4f 0-120 novices' handicap chase at Bangor, rated 116 and quietly supported in the market. Held up in arrears, jumping adequately, he made steady progress approaching the third last and was left clear by a falling rival two fences from home. Drew clear approaching the last and began to pull away, despite pecking, to win by eight lengths.

A huge horse who shaped as if he had more to offer at Bangor and could be the right type for a valuable handicap chase in the autumn.

KING'S SOCKS (6YR BAY GELDING)

TRAINER:	David Pipe
PEDIGREE:	King's Best – Alexandrina (Monsun)
FORM (CHASE):	122/30P -
RATING (CHASE):	139
TRIP:	2m +

Has an interesting background, having raced as a two-year-old in France and winning twice over hurdles and once over fences, including a 2m 2f Listed contest at Enghien in May 2016.

Shaped particularly well in defeat on his next two starts, beaten 11 lengths by Footpad in an extended 2m 3f Grade 3 race and then second to the same horse, beaten two and a half lengths, in a Grade 1 contest at Auteuil.

Subsequently had wind surgery and ran an interesting first race for these connections in an extended 2m 4f graduation chase at Kempton in February, held up despite the slow pace and never a factor, beaten eight lengths on highly unfavourable terms by Modus, receiving 4lb and rated 13lb superior.

Had the look of a long-term plot when well supported to win the Brown Advisory & Merriebelle Stable Plate Handicap Chase from a mark of 140 at the Festival, travelling well for most of the trip and looking a threat to all on the turn for home before fading back to fifth on the run-in.

Lost place at halfway before pulling up on his final start back over two miles at Aintree, always doing a bit too much on the outside of the field before dropping away.

Looks extremely favourably treated if he can reproduce the form he showed with Footpad in France. Has been given a wind operation over the summer.

Optimum trip uncertain, but stayed 2m 3f in France and should get further. Evidently a little delicate but a smooth traveller who is still unexposed and should be able to capitalise from his favourable mark.

MISTER WHITAKER (6YR BAY GELDING)

TRAINER:	Mick Channon
PEDIGREE:	Court Cave – Benbradagh Vard (Le Bavard)
FORM (CHASE):	31211 -
RATING (CHASE):	145
TRIP:	2m 4f +

Very progressive last season with the scope to make further improvement, especially if stepped up in trip.

Second in the first of his two bumpers and third twice from three starts over hurdles before switching to fences last autumn. Ran third on his chase debut at Fontwell before stepping up markedly to beat Solstice Star by two lengths off 118 in a 2m 4f 0-135 novices' chase at Carlisle in November.

Second to Hell's Kitchen from a mark of 125 on Boxing Day at Kempton before beating Theatre Territory over 2m 5f at Cheltenham off 129, idling on the run-in.

Mister Whitaker – could improve beyond handicaps

Well fancied next time off 137 for the Close Brothers Novices' Handicap Chase at Cheltenham. Ridden with great finesse by Brian Hughes, held up just off the pace on the inside of the field throughout, making stealthy progress but still only sixth at the second last before moving up to third approaching the final fence.

Looked held for a few strides before responding positively to his rider's urgings, getting up close home to beat Rather Be by a head.

A deceptive horse in that he only does the minimum required to win, so may have something in hand of his current mark.

A half-brother to useful performers Broadway Buffalo, Ballyboley and Christdalo – all of them effective at three miles.

Can get close to a fence but travels powerfully through a race and doesn't lose momentum. Best suited to reasonable ground.

Could prove very useful over three miles, possibly even superior to handicap class. Has more to offer.

MS PARFOIS (7YR CHESTNUT MARE)

TRAINER:	**Anthony Honeyball**
PEDIGREE:	**Mahler – Dolly Lewis (Sir Harry Lewis)**
FORM (CHASE):	**3111222 -**
RATING (CHASE):	**146**
TRIP:	**3m +**

Admirably game performer; in the first three in 12 of her 14 starts and with the scope to progress to a higher level over fences.

Did well to win a bumper, at Uttoxeter in April 2016, on her debut given her stout pedigree. Highly tried when switched to hurdles, finishing fourth and third in Listed contests before appreciating the drop in grade to win a 2m 5f novices' event at Warwick in January 2017.

Again shaped well next time when third to Colin's Sister in a 2m 4f Grade 2 contest at Sandown before landing short odds when beating three rivals in a novices' contest at Fontwell in March.

Improved for the switch to fences last autumn, displaying great tenacity to beat Theatre Territory by a length over 2m 5f at Cheltenham in December. Showed her toughness by reappearing just five days later in an extended 2m 7f Listed novices' chase at Newbury, again keeping on bravely at the finish to beat Happy Diva, rated 5lb superior, by three and a half lengths.

Stepped up to three miles the following month and beat Duel At Dawn by five lengths in a Listed contest before finding the talented Black Corton too good for her in a 3m Grade 2 contest at Ascot.

Looked sure to prevail next time in the National Hunt Challenge Cup, leading halfway up the run-in before being caught close home by Rathvinden after compromising her chance with a couple of ponderous jumps. No disgrace back

Ms Parfois – admirably game

at 3m 1f at Aintree in April, beaten three and three-quarter lengths by the progressive Terrefort.

Prone to the occasional ponderous jump over a fence and used to pull herself up once in front but a mare of rare courage who is bred to stay forever.

Likely to come into her own in one of the season's midwinter handicaps, with the Welsh Grand National looking an obvious target. A great credit to her trainer.

ON THE BLIND SIDE (6YR BAY GELDING)

TRAINER:	Nicky Henderson
PEDIGREE:	Stowaway – Such A Set Up (Supreme Leader)
FORM (HURDLE):	1110 -
RATING (HURDLE):	151
TRIP:	2m 4f +

Looks set to become one of the season's top novice chasers.

Beat a field packed with subsequent winners on his sole start in a point-to-point at Kilfeacle in January 2017.

Changed hands the following month for £205,000 to join these connections and made his debut in a 2m 4f maiden hurdle at Aintree in October, finding plenty for pressure to beat Another Stowaway by three-quarters of a length, with Aye Aye Charlie eight lengths back in third.

Never travelling all that well the following month in a 2m 5f Grade 2 contest at Cheltenham, fourth and looking beaten turning for home before switching after the last and responding well to pressure to win going away by two and a half lengths.

Did it much more easily next time in an extended 2m 4f novices' hurdle at Sandown, travelling well and coming away approaching the last to beat Springtown Lake easily by nine lengths.

Had to miss Cheltenham due to a problem with a hind leg and reappeared in the Grade 1 Betway Mersey Novices' Hurdle at Aintree, up there in second in the early stages and apparently travelling well before struggling on the final turn for home and fading to finish sixth. Ground may have been softer than ideal after a rushed preparation.

Bred to stay, his sire being a strong influence for stamina and his dam an unraced half-sister to very smart staying hurdler and chaser Knockara Beau.

On The Blind Side – a potential top-notcher over fences

Unlikely to represent great value from a betting perspective in his early races but shaped in the manner of a strong stayer over hurdles and may not be seen at his best until he is stepped up to three miles.

Looks a long-term prospect for either the JLT or RSA at the Festival (20/1 for both).

SAM'S GUNNER (5YR CHESTNUT GELDING)

TRAINER:	Mick Easterby
PEDIGREE:	Black Sam Bellamy – Falcon's Gunner (Gunner B)
FORM (HURDLE):	4/2121P -
RATING:	136
TRIP:	3m +

Very stoutly bred son of Black Sam Bellamy, from the family of top staying chaser Bob Tisdall, with the potential to develop into a long-distance handicap chaser.

Showed a modicum of promise in two runs in bumpers before switching to hurdles, running second at Catterick in January before winning a modest contest over an extended 2m 3f at the same track in February.

Sam's Gunner – a dour stayer

Did well to run second to Taxmeifyoucan over an inadequate two miles 13 days later at Kelso before excelling in the Grade 3 National Hunt Novices' Handicap Hurdle Final at Sandown in March, showing courage in the extreme having been under pressure from the back straight and responding dourly to take the lead approaching the last and win going away by seven lengths from a mark of 125.

Failed to sparkle a month later in Grade 1 company at Aintree, possibly feeling the effects of his hard race at Sandown.

Expected to go chasing and is most emphatically one to have on your side over a distance of ground when the mud is flying. Exceptionally game.

Marten's Latest News

If you want to keep in touch with Marten's latest thoughts ring him on:

0906 150 1555

Selections given in the first minute

Calls charged at £1.50 a minute at all times & your telecom provider will add their own Access Charge. Please contact your provider for their charges.

Telephone & Text Service

A non-premium rate version of this line is available. Please call the office if you'd like to join or order online. The line is an 03 number which is the same as calling a landline and included in a mobile phone package. Marten sends a text message direct each day. Prices also available online.

THE DARK HORSES

The following horses are thought to have the potential to win races or improve further on their performances to date. They are drawn from a wide range of backgrounds and should be noted with the long term in mind.

ADJALI (3YR BAY GELDING)

TRAINER:	Nicky Henderson
PEDIGREE:	Kamsin – Anabasis (High Chaparral)
FORM (HURDLE):	21 - 3
RATING:	None
TRIP:	2m

One of the better juvenile hurdlers in France last spring, running second to subsequent dual winner Beaumec De Houelle on his debut at Auteuil in April.

Beat Fighter Du Seuil just under three weeks later at Compiegne before running third to the aforementioned Beaumec De Houelle in an extended 2m 1f Listed contest at Auteuil in May.

Will have a penalty to carry but has the scope to progress to better things beyond his juvenile hurdle season.

ANNAMIX (5YR GREY GELDING)

TRAINER:	Willie Mullins
PEDIGREE:	Martaline – Tashtiyana (Doyoun)
FORM (HURDLE):	2/
RATING:	None
TRIP:	2m

Missed last season but enjoys a very tall reputation in his yard and currently at the head of the market for the Supreme Novices' Hurdle next March.

Shaped with great promise on his sole start, running subsequent chase winner Mick Taros to two and a half lengths over an extended 2m 1f in heavy ground at Vichy in September 2016.

Was rumoured to be one of the most talented recruits to the yard from France and is confidently expected to reflect that reputation when he appears on the track.

ARROWTOWN (6YR BAY MARE)

TRAINER:	Mick Easterby
PEDIGREE:	Rail Link – Protectress (Hector Protector)
FORM (HURDLE):	Unraced
RATING (HURDLE):	None
TRIP:	2m 4f +

Took a while to lose her maiden certificate on the Flat, running 11 times over three seasons before winning a 1m 4f 0-75 apprentice handicap on heavy ground off 71 at Pontefract in September 2017.

Just failed by a short head to win a better class of race the following month over an extended two miles at York off 74.

Returned this autumn in fine form, running second in a 1m 4f Class 4 at Thirsk (77) before winning the same class of race back there off 78 in September. Successfully defied a 4lb higher mark back on heavy ground in an extended 2m 1f 0-95 at Ayr, relishing the test of stamina.

Apparently not straightforward but reported to have schooled well at home and could have a bright future over timber. Appreciates testing conditions.

Mick Easterby – striding forth

BEYONDTHESTORM (5YR BAY GELDING)

TRAINER:	Nicky Henderson
PEDIGREE:	**Flemensfirth – Blue Gale (Be My Native)**
FORM (PTP):	**1 -**
RATING:	**None**
TRIP:	**2m +**

Displayed a very good attitude to beat subsequent bumper runner-up Presented Well and subsequent point-to-point winner Mayohill in a 3m maiden point-to-point at Moira in December.

Sixth foal and a half-brother to 3m-plus hunter chaser Kimora out of an unraced full sister to bumper winner Culmore Native.

Bought soon after his success for £150,000 and will run in the colours of Cheveley Park.

Has the potential to develop into a useful staying novice hurdler.

BULLS HEAD (6YR BAY GELDING)

TRAINER:	Martin Todhunter
PEDIGREE:	Darsi – Mrs Jenks (Gunner B)
FORM (HURDLE):	0000/112 - 0
RATING (HURDLE):	115
TRIP:	2m 4f +

Patiently campaigned by his former trainer Edward Stanners in Ireland as a novice, beaten an aggregate of 172 lengths in four starts, generally jumping poorly and finishing well in arrears.

Moved to his current trainer and entered for his first handicap from a mark of 102, he landed some hefty bets when winning an extended 2m 0-100 at Newcastle by five lengths, travelling well turning for home and staying on strongly to come home with something in hand.

Followed that up three weeks later from a mark of 108 in an extended 2m 4f 0-140 at Ayr, shuffled along to get upsides before striding out to win going away. Beaten back in trip next time at Newcastle when second off 117 before failing to cope with the rise in class at Aintree in May, finishing ninth of 13 on unsuitably good ground.

Relishes mud and bred to stay, coming from the family of staying chaser Bobby Grant. Expected to go novice chasing but needs to jump fences better than hurdles. One to note when the mud is flying.

CADEYRN (6YR BAY GELDING)

TRAINER:	Michael Scudamore
PEDIGREE:	Flemensfirth – Kapricia Speed (Vertical Speed)
FORM (HURDLE):	04121 -
RATING (HURDLE):	135
TRIP:	2m 6f +

Not an obvious inclusion for this section but showed last season that he has what it takes to win in the deep winter ground.

Won a maiden point-to-point at Horse & Jockey in March 2016, before winning the second of his three bumpers at Chepstow's Christmas meeting later that year. Shaped quite well when switched to hurdles on his return last autumn, running on steadily on his second start at Chepstow, before showing his appreciation of a step up in trip when beating Bob Mahler in a 2m 6f novice hurdle at Newcastle, battling on dourly despite clumsy jumps at the last two flights.

Michael Scudamore – does well with his team

Ended the season with a similar effort in heavy ground at Uttoxeter, stepped up to an extended 2m 7f and appreciating every yard of the trip to win by three lengths from I Just Know.

Half-brother to useful stayer Barney Dwan from the family of top two-mile hurdler Geos.

Has a pronounced knee action and is now established as a confirmed mudlark. Not a particularly fluent jumper of hurdles but likely to take better to fences.

One to have on your side in hock-deep conditions but, in the longer term, worth keeping in mind for a Welsh Grand National.

Likeable and very gutsy.

CHAMP (6YR BAY GELDING)

TRAINER:	Nicky Henderson
PEDIGREE:	King's Theatre – China Sky (Definite Article)
FORM (HURDLE):	2 - 11
RATING (HURDLE):	139
TRIP:	2m 4f

Probably better than his summer form suggests, having won a maiden hurdle at odds of 1/14 at Perth in May from subsequent winner Court Dreaming and then again over 2m 5f at Warwick.

Had shaped well when winning and second in two bumpers before running Vinndication to a neck in an extended 2m 5f novices' hurdle at Ascot in January.

Remains a novice over hurdles for the current season. Has a strong bias in his pedigree to good ground.

CHANTE NEIGE (4YR BAY FILLY)

TRAINER:	Willie Mullins
PEDIGREE:	Martaline – Russian Taiga (Turgeon)
FORM (HURDLE):	3/
RATING:	None
TRIP:	2m

Ran third on her sole racecourse appearance in a conditions contest for unraced horses at Auteuil in March 2017. Race won by Santa Adelia, a winner again next time, from Stormy Ireland, a subsequent Listed winner over hurdles for this trainer.

Off the track last season due to a setback but reported to be in top form and expected to take high rank in mares' novice hurdles. Shows talent in her work.

Willie Mullins – in customary pose

CLARENDON STREET (5YR BAY GELDING)

TRAINER:	Nicky Henderson
PEDIGREE:	Court Cave – Carrigeen Kalmia (Norwich)
FORM (BUMPER):	4 -
RATING:	None
TRIP:	2m +

One of the most interesting prospects in this section.

Made his sole start for trainer Emmet Mullins in a Punchestown bumper in April, held up in arrears throughout and never asked to improve his position at any stage, going wide around the home turn and finishing strongly into fourth under minimal encouragement from his amateur rider.

Form held up well, with the third winning his next two races.

First foal of a useful chaser up to 2m 4f, a half-sister to fair performer Listed-placed Carrigeen Victor, staying hurdler and chaser Caduceus from the family of Irish National winner Rogue Angel.

Hard to assess on the evidence of his one run but was eye-catching in the extreme and is sure to improve for the move to his new yard.

DOWNTOWN GETAWAY (5YR BAY GELDING)

TRAINER:	Nicky Henderson
PEDIGREE:	Getaway – Shang A Lang (Commander Collins)
FORM (BUMPER):	1 -
RATING:	None
TRIP:	2m 4f

Looked a staying sort when striding away to win what turned out to be a useful bumper on his sole start at Fairyhouse last December.

Starting at 14/1, was always handy just off the leaders until leading over two furlongs out and pulling well clear to beat Remastered by 12 lengths. Runner-up has since won a bumper for David Pipe, third has won a bumper for Joseph O'Brien and fourth has won a maiden hurdle for Noel Meade. Others further back have since run well.

Promising sort for staying novice hurdles.

EL BARRA (4YR BROWN GELDING)

TRAINER:	**Willie Mullins**
PEDIGREE:	**Racinger – Oasaka (Robin Des Champs)**
FORM (PTP):	**2 -**
RATING:	**None**
TRIP:	**2m 4f +**

Ridden with an eye to the future when chasing home Fury Road in a 4yo maiden point-to-point at Dromahane in May.

Nicely bred, fourth foal and a half-brother to useful hurdler and chaser Barra out of an unraced half-sister to 2m 5f winning hurdler Liberia. Sire was a Group-winning miler in France who has notably produced Barman, winner of seven races for Nicky Henderson.

Subsequently acquired for £280,000 at Cheltenham in May to run in the colours of Susannah and Rich Ricci.

Rated by those close to him as a horse of great potential.

EL KALDOUN (4YR BAY GELDING)

TRAINER:	Nicky Henderson
PEDIGREE:	Special Kaldoun – Kermesse d'Estruval (Cadoudal)
FORM:	Unraced
RATING:	None
TRIP:	2m

Unraced son of multiple Group 2 and 3 winner Special Kaldoun and a half-brother to a handful of winners including five-race winner Rival D'Estruval, winner of three races over hurdles and twice over fences for owner Raymond Anderson Green.

Shaped very well on the gallops when last seen without making it to the track. One of the more promising unraced horses in his yard.

ELYSEES (3YR CHESTNUT GELDING)

TRAINER:	Alan King
PEDIGREE:	Champs Elysees – Queen Of Tara (Sadler's Wells)
FORM (FLAT):	0041013034
RATING (FLAT):	78
TRIP:	2m +

Shaped well in three educational runs over a trip short of his requirements before winning a 1m 4f 0-65 from an opening mark of 66 at Wolverhampton in April.

Won again two starts later from a mark of 70 in a 1m 6f 0-70 at Sandown and has sustained that level of form despite failing to win in four subsequent starts, the last three off 78.

Shaped particularly well on his most recent outing in an extended 2m 0-80 at York, keeping on strongly despite having raced keenly in the early stages.

In very good hands for juvenile hurdling and reported to have schooled well at home.

Alan King – does well with his juvenile hurdlers

EPATANTE (4YR BAY FILLY)

TRAINER:	Nicky Henderson
PEDIGREE:	No Risk At All – Kadjara (Silver Rainbow)
FORM (BUMPER):	211 -
RATING:	None
TRIP:	2m

One of the most exciting fillies to race in France last season.

Runner-up to Extra Noire on her debut at Saint-Malo in August, she then beat Enivrante Passion by six lengths at Le Lion D'Angers, quickening away to win with something in hand.

Final start came in the Grade 1 Prix Jacques de Vienne at Saint-Cloud, pulling clear to beat previous winner Eveilduboulay, with subsequent winner El Martel a further nine lengths back in third.

Ninth foal and a half-sister to useful bumper and hurdle winner Tante Sissi and other winners over hurdles and fences.

Apparently acquired by JP McManus and looks sure to be the centre of attention when she appears. Probably very useful.

FAUSTINOVICK (4YR BAY GELDING)

TRAINER:	Colin Tizzard
PEDIGREE:	Black Sam Bellamy – Cormorant Cove (Fair Mix)
FORM (PTP):	2
RATING:	None
TRIP:	2m 4f +

Left the impression he had much more to give when runner-up to subsequent £330,000 purchase Andy Dufresne at Borris House on his sole point-to-point start in March.

Given a patient ride by Derek O'Connor he moved up to challenge approaching the third last before the winner found a change of gear to pull away and win by six lengths.

Subsequently bought for £170,000 at the Goffs Aintree Sale.

First foal of an unraced half-sister to Flat winners at around a mile from the family of Group 1 winner Cormorant Wood, top-class hurdler River Ceiriog and the family of Inglis Drever.

Has joined a trainer who takes his time, so probably more one for novice chasing but could still be interesting along the way over hurdles.

GALLAHERS CROSS (6YR BAY GELDING)

TRAINER:	**Nicky Henderson**
PEDIGREE:	**Getaway – Raheen Lady (Oscar)**
FORM (BUMPER):	**14 -**
RATING:	**None**
TRIP:	**2m 4f**

Progressive late-maturing sort with a long-term future.

Beat subsequent winner Double You Be on his sole start in a 5yo maiden point-to-point at Punchestown in February 2017.

Appeared in a bumper at Galway in October and responded gamely to strong pressure, coming between horses on the home turn to beat Monstrosity by six and a half lengths.

Subsequently bought by these connections for £260,000 and appeared in a decent Listed bumper at Ascot, travelling well throughout before looking one-paced two furlongs from home. Stayed on again in the closing stages to finish fourth to Didtheyleaveuoutto and Bullionaire.

Second foal and a half-brother to point-to-point winner Call Of The Loon out of an unraced half-sister to the useful Lord

Strickland and Mill O'The Rag from the family of Hansel Rag.

Looks as if he will need at least two and a half miles to show his form, but could not be in better hands for a horse with his long-term potential.

GOSHEVEN (5YR BAY GELDING)

TRAINER:	Philip Hobbs
PEDIGREE:	Presenting – Fair Choice (Zaffaran)
FORM (HURDLE):	30 -
RATING:	None
TRIP:	2m 4f +

An obvious inclusion for any 'notebook' last season given the eye-catching manner of his performances in a bumper and over hurdles.

Made his debut in a Wincanton bumper on Boxing Day, bustled along from halfway and stayed on steadily to finish a never-nearer fifth, beaten 21 lengths by the winner.

Switched to hurdles in March for a 2m 5f novice event at Kempton and ran in a similar manner, behind in the first half of the race – occasionally giving the hurdles too much air – before plugging on in good style to finish third.

Shaped even better on his third run of the season, raised in grade for a Class 2 novices' hurdle over an extended 2m 4f at Cheltenham, again settled in arrears and overjumping at times, before making stealthy headway turning for home and staying on to finish fifth, beaten just under seven lengths by the promising and highly tried Diese Des Bieffes.

Fifth foal and a half-brother to 3m chase and hurdle winners Vesper Bell and Aurora Bell. Dam a half-sister to bumper and 3m chase winner Commanche Hero from a good jumping family.

Looks like a long-term chasing prospect but will be eligible for handicaps after one more run and could prove very effective in staying novice handicap hurdles.

Shaped with great promise last season and undoubtedly has more to offer. Bred to stay well.

HEATSTROKE (6YR BAY GELDING)

TRAINER:	Nicky Henderson
PEDIGREE:	Galileo – Walklikeanegyptian (Danehill)
FORM (FLAT):	01/40/0 -
RATING (FLAT):	85
TRIP:	2m

Comes with risks attached, having had a truncated career on the Flat with Charlie Hills and running just five times in three seasons.

Caught the eye in a major way when quickening from way off the pace to beat 11 rivals in a 1m maiden on the all-weather surface at Kempton in October 2014. Looked a colt of top-class potential at the time but missed the entirety of 2015 and did not reappear until May 2016, running fourth off a mark of 87 in a 1m 0-95 at Sandown.

Showed a similar level of form on his only other start that season at Yarmouth in July. Not seen out again until April 2017, again staying on steadily at the finish in an extended 1m 0-95 at Nottingham.

Intriguing to learn that he has joined this top trainer, strongly suggesting that connections retain their faith in him.

Evidently not an easy horse to train, but looked a potential top-notcher in his maiden and could be very useful if he can be kept sound.

Nicky Henderson – enjoying a quiet ride

KING ROLAND (4YR BROWN GELDING)

TRAINER:	Harry Fry
PEDIGREE:	Stowaway – Kiltiernan Robin (Robin Des Champs)
FORM (PTP):	1
RATING:	None
TRIP:	2m 4f

First foal of an unraced half-sister to French 2m 7f chase winner Brise Du Large from the family of long-distance chase winner Zimbabwe.

Impressed when winning a 3m maiden point-to-point at Larkhill in April, coming up against the useful Foxworthy. Held up on the rail by Tommie O'Brien, he was left clear when market rival Foxworthy made an error at the third from home. Found an impressive turn of foot to quicken clear on the run-in and win by 10 lengths, taking another quarter-mile to pull up.

Tommie O'Brien said afterwards that the performance was as good as any he has seen in his 10 years of pointing experience. Subsequently sold privately to these connections.

Will be given time to find his feet but has the pace to run creditably in a bumper. Very exciting.

LOUGH DERG SPIRIT (6YR BAY GELDING)

TRAINER:	**Nicky Henderson**
PEDIGREE:	**Westerner – Sno-Cat Lady (Executive Perk)**
FORM (HURDLE):	**141P/2000 -**
RATING (HURDLE):	**136**
TRIP:	**2m +**

First caught the eye with his super-slick hurdling as a novice in 2016/17, winning two of his four starts at Kempton and Musselburgh.

Began last season with a creditable effort in second to London Prize from a mark of 137 in the Elite Hurdle at Wincanton, doing well in trying to concede the useful but ill-fated winner 3lb.

Shaped better than his finishing position suggests when sixth of 24 to Kalashnikov in the prestigious Betfair Hurdle at Newbury (138). Ran a similar race next time in the Martin Pipe Conditional Jockeys' Handicap Hurdle at Cheltenham, sticking on well at the finish despite unsuitably testing ground.

Ran below that level of form on his final start at Sandown (137).

Rated better than his hurdling form suggests, having run very creditably in two of the season's top handicap hurdles despite encountering unfavourable ground. Would have been seen in a far better light had conditions not been as testing.

Has a chance to show his true talent on better going this season. Will be sent chasing and if he jumps fences as well as he did hurdles then he could go far.

Very interesting and still unexposed.

MAGIC SAINT (4YR BAY GELDING)

TRAINER:	Paul Nicholls
PEDIGREE:	Saint Des Saints – Magic Poline (Trempolino)
FORM (CHASE):	1135 -
RATING (CHASE):	145
TRIP:	2m 4f +

Winning hurdler and chaser in France, landing a 2m 2f three-year-old hurdle at Auteuil in September 2017 by a neck and again there in October by a head from Mozo Guapo, winner in August of a Listed race over hurdles.

Made a successful transition to chasing, winning at Auteuil in November and then again in March, before running third to Spanish One, subsequently not disgraced in Grade 1 and 2 company. Last time well beaten when stepped up to 2m 6f in April.

Has already shown he is useful and has the youth to move further forward.

May be the type to run in handicap chases with the four-year-old allowance.

THE DARK HORSES | **43**

Auteuil – where it all begins for so many

MASTER TOMMYTUCKER (7YR BAY GELDING)

TRAINER:	**Paul Nicholls**
PEDIGREE:	**Kayf Tara – No Need For Alarm (Romany Rye)**
FORM (HURDLE):	**11 -**
RATING (HURDLE):	**143**
TRIP:	**2m 4f +**

Did well to overcome greenness and a last-flight blunder, costing him the lead and momentum, when battling back bravely on his debut to beat subsequent winner Molineaux in an extended 2m 2f novices' hurdle at Exeter in February.

Returned there just under two months later to beat King Calvin, then rated on 134, with great ease stepped up to an extended 2m 5f, always travelling well within himself and winning without coming off the bridle.

Probably reasonably treated on 143 and may run from that mark over hurdles, but the plan is to switch him to fences sooner rather than later.

NEBUCHADNEZZAR (3YR BAY GELDING)

TRAINER:	**Alan King**
PEDIGREE:	**Planteur – Trexana (Kaldoun)**
FORM (FLAT):	**044 - 43**
RATING (FLAT):	**69**
TRIP:	**2m +**

Shaped well in three fair-class maidens at two, performing in the manner of a potential staying handicapper.

Has run fairly well in two starts this season, last of four to Westbrook Bertie from a mark of 71 in a 1m 2f 0-85 at Salisbury in April, and then when third of 12 to Pippin off 69 in a 1m 4f 0-70 at Newbury in June.

May have found the conditions too fast on the latter occasion and has been rested and saved for softer ground later this autumn.

Appeals as a horse with much more to offer, both on the Flat and as a juvenile hurdler.

NEVER ADAPT (3YR CHESTNUT FILLY)

TRAINER:	Nicky Henderson
PEDIGREE:	Anabaa Blue – She Hates Me (Hawk Wing)
FORM (HURDLE):	1
RATING:	None
TRIP:	2m

A useful sort who can take advantage of the fillies' allowance in high-class juvenile hurdles.

Winner of her sole start last season, making all to take a 2m hurdle in heavy ground at Compiegne by 10 lengths. Form subsequently shown to be only moderate.

Still eligible for juvenile hurdles. Needs to learn to relax but not short of talent and looks the type that could set up a sequence.

ON A PROMISE (6YR GREY GELDING)

TRAINER:	Nicky Richards
PEDIGREE:	Definite Article – Silvers Promise (Presenting)
FORM (HURDLE):	0000/1121 -
RATING (HURDLE):	120
TRIP:	3m

Cannily campaigned in his early days, beaten an aggregate of 178 lengths in his first four runs over hurdles, on the last occasion off 98 in an extended 2m handicap hurdle at Newcastle.

Evidently did not catch connections unawares on his seasonal return in November, stepped up to an extended 2m 5f and rated on 91, heavily supported at double-figure odds down to 7/2 and stayed on strongly after taking the lead at the second-last flight.

Stepped up to an extended 2m 7f a week later at Hexham and won off the same mark, drawing clear to win by four lengths. Found the well-treated Pop Rockstar too good for him just under a month later in a 3m 0-110 at Wetherby (105).

Rested until late March, returned in a 2m 7f 0-120 at Market Rasen and overcame a mistake at the last to win by five lengths.

Raised 29lb through the course of the season and still looked on the upward curve on his latest start. Acts well on good ground and looks an ideal type for novice chasing.

ROBIN ROE (7YR BAY GELDING)

Trainer:	Olly Murphy
PEDIGREE:	Robin Des Champs – Talktothetail (Flemensfirth)
FORM (HURDLE):	1F/
RATING (HURDLE):	None
TRIP:	2m 4f +

Comes with risks having been off the track since December 2016, but was very promising when last seen for Dan Skelton and warrants the time that connections have invested in his recovery.

Runner-up on his point-to-point debut at Loughbrickland in March 2015 and then beat Laser Light, now a useful hurdler with Alan King, at Boulta in November of that year.

Made his debut under Rules for former trainer Dan Skelton when beating 17 rivals in a bumper at Warwick in March 2016. Next appeared in a 2m 4f maiden hurdle at Aintree, pulling away to beat No Comment impressively by 12 lengths. Stepped up in class next time for the Grade 1 Challow Hurdle at

Newbury, travelling well when falling three flights from home.

Has apparently been back in work for a while and has the ability to go a long way if he can be kept sound. Has the option of building on his form over hurdles or switching to chasing. Could prove very useful if all goes well.

SAM'S ADVENTURE (6YR BAY GELDING)

TRAINER:	**Brian Ellison**
PEDIGREE:	**Black Sam Bellamy – My Adventure (Strong Gale)**
FORM (BUMPER):	**11/21/**
RATING:	**None**
TRIP:	**2m 4f +**

One of the best bumper performers around in the last two seasons and expected to prove a useful recruit to hurdles if he stays right.

Hacked up in a Wetherby bumper on heavy ground in February 2016, coming home on the bridle eased down. Did very well just under a month later to beat Bags Groove by a nose in the DBS Spring Sales Bumper at Newbury, with useful sorts stretched out behind.

No disgrace the following December when beaten a short head by Better Getalong at Ayr, trying to concede the winner 8lb, before returning to winning ways back there in January when beating Mcgowan's Pass, subsequently a winner of a bumper and over hurdles, by three lengths, giving the runner-up 10lb.

The 13th foal of her dam and closely related to staying performers Eight Is My Number and Kayf Adventure.

Bred to stay well and evidently loves the mud. Has the potential to develop into a useful staying hurdler.

SEBASTOPOL (4YR BAY GELDING)

TRAINER:	**Tom Lacey**
PEDIGREE:	**Fame And Glory – Knockcroghery (Pelder)**
FORM (BUMPER):	**1 -**
RATING:	**None**
TRIP:	**2m**

Winner by 15 lengths of an open maiden at Larkhill on his sole start in a point-to-point in January 2018.

Tom Lacey – creating a very good impression

Well supported to make a successful racecourse debut in an Ayr bumper in April 2018 and duly delivered, a little keen early on but travelling well to challenge in the straight and quickening clear to beat dual winner Black Pirate by three and three-quarter lengths.

Appears to have a turn of foot and expected to be competitive at a decent level for his talented handler.

SILVER FOREVER (4YR GREY FILLY)

TRAINER:	Paul Nicholls
PEDIGREE:	Jeremy – Silver Prayer (Roselier)
FORM (PTP):	1
RATING:	None
TRIP:	2m +

Beat Annie Mc easily by 10 lengths on her sole start last season in a 4yo mares' maiden point-to-point at Bartlemy in May.

Seventh foal and a half-sister to staying chase winners Ruapehu and Crown Hill out of an unraced full sister to 3m 1f winner The Manse Brae from the family of Mary's Manna.

Expected to appreciate a distance of ground but will be placed effectively by her handler to take full advantage of the mares' allowance.

STYLE DE VOLE (3YR GREY GELDING)

TRAINER:	Nicky Henderson
PEDIGREE:	Vol De Nuit – Anowe De Jelois (Red Guest)
FORM (FLAT):	1
RATING:	None
TRIP:	2m

Acquired after winning a maiden for unraced horses by five lengths over an extended 1m 2f at Saint-Cloud in June for trainer Yannick Fouin. Form relatively untested thereafter but could hardly have looked more impressive.

Second foal and a half-brother to useful dual-winning hurdler Style De Garde, also in this yard, out of a winning hurdler and chaser from a family that traces back to 3m 2f performer Bobble Hat Bob.

Acquired for JP McManus and rated one of the most promising juveniles in the yard.

SURF WALK (3YR BAY GELDING)

TRAINER:	Nicky Henderson
PEDIGREE:	Born To Sea – Meon Mix (Kayf Tara)
FORM:	Unraced
RATING:	None
TRIP:	2m

Could be the type to win one of the valuable sales bumper races.

By Born To Sea, a half-brother to Sea The Stars, and a half-brother to Jessica Harrington's Flat and hurdle winner (Listed placed) Holding Pattern, dual Flat winner Sublimation and five-race Flat winner Metronomic.

Described as an exceptional mover when bought at the Land Rover Sale and bred to have pace. One to note on his debut.

TEDHAM (4YR BAY GELDING)

TRAINER:	Jonjo O'Neill
PEDIGREE:	Shirocco – Alegralil (King's Theatre)
FORM:	3 -
RATING:	None
TRIP:	2m +

Not an obvious inclusion for this section but there was a very strong word for this son of Shirocco before his debut and he ran well to finish third in a decent contest.

Second foal of a winner up to 2m 3f over hurdles from the family of Theatrical Star.

Was very green on his debut and may make above-average improvement.

THE BIG GALLOPER (4YR CHESTNUT GELDING)

TRAINER:	Charles Byrnes
PEDIGREE:	Mahler – Cuiloge Lady (Beneficial)
FORM (HURDLE):	0 -
RATING:	None
TRIP:	2m 4f +

A big raw horse but has already shown enough to suggest he will win races for his shrewd handler.

Showed plenty of pace under a positive ride on his debut in a Leopardstown bumper in March. Plugged on steadily to finish second to Feelin' Groovy 10 days later in a bumper at Limerick.

Never put into the race on his hurdling debut at Cork in April, staying on steadily from arrears to finish a distant fifth of 15.

Half-brother to 3m 1f chase winner What A Moment out of an unraced half-sister to staying hurdler/chaser Seven Is My Number.

Bred to stay and evidently being brought along quietly with the long term in mind. One to monitor closely for a low-grade staying handicap hurdle, especially when the money is down.

TOPOFTHEGAME (6YR CHESTNUT GELDING)

TRAINER:	**Paul Nicholls**
PEDIGREE:	**Flemensfirth – Derry Vale (Mister Lord)**
FORM (HURDLE):	**142/412 -**
RATING (HURDLE):	**154**
TRIP:	**2m 6f +**

Very interesting chasing prospect with the potential to go a long way up the ladder.

Made all and quickened away to beat No Hassle Hoff and Brave Eagle, both now useful under Rules, in a point-to-point at Belclare in March 2016.

Made a successful hurdling debut for this trainer over an extended 2m 5f at Ascot in December 2016, before running fourth in a Grade 2 contest at Cheltenham in January. Second to Beyond Conceit the following month at Ascot.

Fell when travelling well in a beginners' chase on his seasonal return at Newbury in November. Switched back to hurdling for the remainder of the season, running well from a mark of 139 when fourth in the Lanzarote Hurdle at Kempton in January.

Looked useful the following month when winning a Grade 3 over an extended 2m 7f at Sandown from a mark of 142 before going down by a neck to Bleu Berry off 150 in the 2m 5f Coral Cup at Cheltenham.

Was given plenty of light in his races last season, usually ridden around the outside, and tended to dive at the hurdles but showed a good attitude at the finish and clearly stays well.

Has the credentials to make a top novice chaser provided he enjoys a better experience than on his last attempt over fences.

UMNDENI (4YR BAY GELDING)

TRAINER:	**Philip Hobbs**
PEDIGREE:	**Balko – Marie Royale (Turgeon)**
FORM (BUMPER):	**1**
RATING:	**None**
TRIP:	**2m 4f**

Could develop into one of the season's better novice hurdlers.

Had been working well at home prior to his debut in a 17-runner bumper at Warwick in April. Took up the running four furlongs from home and stayed on strongly in the closing stages to beat Newbury bumper winner Morning Vicar by two and three-quarter lengths with the well-regarded Tedham back in third.

Cost €175,000 as a three-year-old and a full brother to useful hurdler Vision Des Flos out of a half-sister to the useful chaser Balko Des Flos and the talented but delicate Salut Flo.

Comes from a top-class family and could not have made a better start to his career. Expected to make a big impression at a decent level.

JOIN US!

Since 1980 we have managed Clubs and Partnerships!

In November 2017 we launched our most recent Club (which costs our members £40 per month) and we have been very happy with how things have gone so far.

We have had a number of requests to start another one so we are busily preparing for our next Club.

If you are not already registered for information on our racehorse ownership opportunities please contact us to be added to our list.

Please include any preferences you may have or trainers you think we should consider.

Rebecca

Twitter: @racingdarkhorse

Dark Horse Racing, 69 Highgate, Kendal LA9 4ED

Telephone: 01539 736836

Email: rebecca@darkhorseracing.com

THE DARK HANDICAPPERS

The following horses appear to have been prepared with handicaps in mind or may have something in hand of their current handicap marks.

AIR DE ROCK (6YR BAY GELDING)

TRAINER:	Venetia Williams
PEDIGREE:	High Rock – Onciale (Ultimately Lucky)
FORM (CHASE):	0 -
RATING (CHASE):	102
TRIP:	2m 4f

Very unexposed, having run nine times over hurdles and just once over fences.

Showed ability in four runs in France as a three- and four-year-old, running fourth twice and third once, before moving to this yard in October 2016.

Displayed precious little ability in five starts over hurdles, dropping from a mark of 115 to 108. Made the switch to chasing last autumn and finished fifth of nine in a 2m 0-125 novices' handicap chase at Chepstow.

Not seen out again but would not still be in this yard if his current mark were deemed an accurate reflection of his ability.

BEHIND TIME (7YR BAY GELDING)

TRAINER:	Harry Fry
PEDIGREE:	Stowaway – She's Got To Go (Glacial Storm)
FORM (CHASE):	034231PP -
RATING (CHASE):	126
TRIP:	3m

Probably not without his limitations but tends to pop up when wanted, notably when landing some serious wagers in an extended 2m 5f conditional jockeys' handicap from a mark of 115 in November 2016.

Harry Fry – may have some fun with Behind Time

Patchy form since then over both hurdles and fences, but ridden with an eye to the future over a trip short of his requirements in his first three starts over fences, notably catching the eye when last of four at Plumpton in December.

Stepped up to a more appropriate 2m 4f for his handicap chase debut at Wincanton in January and ran a close second to Speedalong from a mark of 120, keeping on well at the finish after being left with a lot to do.

Improved again up to three miles in heavy ground at Ffos Las, staying on into third from a mark of 120, before winning a 3m Class 2 handicap chase at Uttoxeter in March, equipped with sheepskin cheekpieces for the first time.

May have found the race coming too soon, having made mistakes, when pulled up a fortnight later at Haydock. Pulled up again next time at Ffos Las.

Bred to stay extreme distances but needs to brush up his jumping if he is to improve. Undeniably has ability and leaves the strong impression there may be better to come. Relishes testing ground.

HUNTERS CALL (8YR BAY GELDING)

TRAINER:	**Olly Murphy**
PEDIGREE:	**Medaaly – Accordiontogelica (Accordion)**
FORM (HURDLE):	**1/04030/4031 -**
RATING (HURDLE):	**137**
TRIP:	**2m +**

A top-class handicap hurdler when on song, as he proved when winning the Racing Welfare Handicap Hurdle by three lengths from a mark of 128 on his first run for this trainer at Ascot in December 2017.

Olly Murphy – still on an upward curve

Had previously been performing consistently though without great success at a lower level in Ireland, often competitive until weakening or being found short of pace in the closing stages.

Raised 9lb from 128 to 137 after his Ascot success but still expected to prove competitive by his handler from his new mark.

Lightly raced with the scope to improve, especially if stepped up beyond two miles. One to note for the Greatwood Hurdle and another crack at the race he won at Ascot.

IFANDABUT (6YR BAY GELDING)

TRAINER:	Venetia Williams
PEDIGREE:	Scorpion – Native Wonder (Good Thyne)
FORM (HURDLE):	000 -
RATING (HURDLE):	94
TRIP:	2m 4f

Has been beaten over 250 lengths in his three starts over hurdles but would not still be in the yard if this were an accurate measure of his ability.

Venetia Williams – hoping for a better season

Third foal of a point-to-point-winning half-sister to fair hurdle/chase winner Hangover from the family of top chaser Strong Promise.

Looks mediocre at best but worth a quiet look for market interest in a low-grade handicap.

JUST MINDED (7YR BAY GELDING)

TRAINER:	**Olly Murphy**
PEDIGREE:	**Kayf Tara – Georgia On My Mind (Belmez)**
FORM (CHASE):	**FP342 -**
RATING (CHASE):	**118**
TRIP:	**2m 4f +**

Impressed physically and with his attitude when winning a bumper at Carlisle in November 2016 for former handler Sue Smith. Had a hard race that day and possibly felt the effects for quite a while, never really progressing in the manner expected. Ran well on occasions, notably when winning a novices' hurdle at Market Rasen in March 2017, but didn't make the anticipated progress when switched to chasing last season.

Showed little promise when failing to complete on his first two starts before finishing a distant third of four from a mark of 119 in a 3m 1f novices' handicap chase at Catterick. Looked thoroughly out of love with the game next time at Market Rasen before showing a glimmer of hope on his final start at Sedgefield, second over an extended 2m 3f.

Has subsequently joined a trainer with a reputation for rekindling the enthusiasm of jaded sorts.

Certainly had the potential early in his career to prove useful and worth keeping an eye on in novice handicap chases, especially when strong in the market.

MASTER BLUEYES (5YR GREY GELDING)

TRAINER:	**Alan King**
PEDIGREE:	**Mastercraftsman – Miss Blueyes (Dushyantor)**
FORM (HURDLE):	**422110/**
RATING (HURDLE):	**150**
TRIP:	**2m +**

Consistent and very likeable performer both on the Flat and over hurdles.

Ran eight times on the Flat, three times at two and then stepped up to middle distances to win handicaps off 72 and 79 before shaping well in better events off 83 and 84.

Switched to hurdling in October 2016, but raced keenly and ran fourth on his debut and then second twice at Kempton and Huntingdon. Beat Long Call by 18 lengths at Ludlow in February 2017 and then landed the Grade 2 Adonis Juvenile Hurdle at Kempton by 11 lengths before finishing tenth to Defi Du Seuil in the Triumph Hurdle, pulling up lame.

A case of unfinished business with this versatile performer, who has the ability to win one of the season's top handicap hurdles, assuming he can be kept right.

NO COMMENT (7YR BROWN GELDING)

TRAINER:	Philip Hobbs
PEDIGREE:	Kayf Tara – Dizzy Frizzy (Loup Sauvage)
FORM (CHASE):	30 -
RATING (CHASE):	139
TRIP:	3m

A useful hurdler, winning three and runner-up four times from nine starts, notably landing a hat-trick in 2016/17 when winning at Market Rasen and twice at Plumpton.

Shaped well that season when seventh of 23 to Champagne Classic in the Martin Pipe Conditional Jockeys' Handicap Hurdle at Cheltenham and then second in competitive handicap hurdles, stepped up to three miles, at Aintree and Punchestown.

Kayf Tara – a great sire

Ran a race full of promise on his chase debut in the Grade 1 Scilly Isles Novices' Chase at Sandown, up against the very useful Terrefort and Cyrname, and jumping adequately under a considerate ride.

Appeared next in the National Hunt Challenge Cup at Cheltenham, ridden by Derek O'Connor, and evidently fancied to go close.

Held up a long way behind, made steady headway on the final circuit to reach a challenging position on the descent for home only for his run to peter out to drop back into sixth, beaten 58 lengths.

First foal of an unraced half-sister to very useful hurdle and chase winner up to 2m 4f Aran Concerto and other winners at the same trip from the family of top performer Run For Free.

May not have stayed the four miles at Cheltenham but was possibly not at his best, in common with other horses at that time from the yard. Rated 6lb lower over fences than hurdles and could be ideally weighted for one of the season's top handicap chases.

Leaves the distinct impression that his best is yet to come.

OFF YOU GO (5YR BAY GELDING)

TRAINER:	**Charles Byrnes**
PEDIGREE:	**Presenting – Ozzy Oscar (Oscar)**
FORM (HURDLE):	**400311 -**
RATING (HURDLE):	**134**
TRIP:	**2m +**

May not be as exposed as his recent form figures would suggest.

Brought along with the patience characteristic of his trainer in his early runs, showing a level of ability in maiden hurdles in

2017 at Roscommon in June, Punchestown in October and Cork in November.

Finished third from a mark of 105 on his handicap debut in an 80-116 over an extended 2m 4f at Thurles in November. Raised 2lb to 107 and won a 2m 4f handicap hurdle at Limerick over Christmas before showing marked improvement from a mark of 123 to beat 27 rivals in a valuable 2m 0-150 handicap hurdle at Leopardstown in February, showing great tenacity to hold the determined challenge of the runner-up Deal D'estruval after the last.

Raised to 134 but not seen out again.

Second foal of an unraced half-sister to a winner up to 2m 6f from the family of Irish National winner Shutthefrontdoor.

Has the scope and pedigree to improve again when stepped up in trip. Handled heavy ground very well last season and looks the right type for one of the season's top staying handicaps.

Sure to be placed to great effect by his canny handler.

THAT'S LIFE (6YR BAY GELDING)

TRAINER:	**Nicky Richards**
PEDIGREE:	**Presenting – Leader's Hall (Saddlers' Hall)**
FORM (HURDLE):	**00PF -**
RATING (HURDLE):	**81**
TRIP:	**2m +**

Very hard to respect on the evidence to date, beaten a total of 213 lengths in his first three starts and then pulled up at Bangor in March and falling two hurdles out when way behind on his final outing at Perth in April.

Has the physique of a far better performer than his form would suggest, having cost €45,000 as a three-year-old store. Nicely bred, being a full brother to Pressies Girl, She's Da One and Burndown – all winners at around two and a half miles. Dam a winning point-to-pointer.

Has a lowly rating but would not still be in the yard if that were an accurate reflection of his potential.

Looks the part and most emphatically one to note for market interest when he appears in a staying handicap hurdle.

THE GREAT GETAWAY (6YR BAY GELDING)

TRAINER:	**Donald McCain**
PEDIGREE:	**Getaway – Park Mist (Great Palm)**
FORM (HURDLE):	**1 -**
RATING (HURDLE):	**118**
TRIP:	**2m 4f +**

Fair performer in Irish point-to-points in 2016/17, running third to subsequent top-class hurdler Getabird on his debut at Largy in April 2016, and then third again and fifth before winning at Curraghmore a year later in April 2017.

Made his debut for this yard in a bumper at Ayr in November before switching to hurdles and staying on gamely to beat Silva Eclipse in an extended 2m 4f novices' hurdle at Newcastle in late December.

Fourth foal of an unraced half-sister to the very useful staying hurdler and chaser Gallant Oscar from the family of top-class performer The Listener.

Reckoned to be favourably treated on his mark but may take advantage of it in a novices' handicap chase. Looked a thorough stayer at Newcastle.

TURNING GOLD (4YR CHESTNUT GELDING)

TRAINER:	Nigel Twiston-Davies
PEDIGREE:	Pivotal – Illusion (Anabaa)
FORM (HURDLE):	224100 -
RATING (HURDLE):	123
TRIP:	2m +

A slow developer on the Flat with Sir Mark Prescott, beaten on his first six starts before winning twice over a mile off 61 and 67 and ending his campaign on a mark of 79.

Has taken a while to adjust to hurdling, second in modest company at Wetherby and Catterick and then fourth at Doncaster before beating Cornerstone Lad by a nose in heavy ground at Haydock in the Victor Ludorum Juvenile Hurdle, not always fluent but rallying gamely to lead on the line.

Raised significantly in class next time to run off 127 in the Fred Winter Juvenile Handicap Hurdle at Cheltenham, racing prominently and having every chance until dropping away to finish a creditable fifth of 22.

Shaped less well on his final start at Ascot, beating one home in a 2m juvenile handicap hurdle.

Kept on bravely up the hill when fifth at Cheltenham in a manner suggesting he has the ability to win a decent handicap hurdle, especially now rated 4lb lower. Acts well on testing ground and may stay beyond two miles.

Nigel Twiston-Davies – could land a decent handicap with Turning Gold

the Weekend card

Informative and insightful news & views

Published weekly every Thursday containing news from our team.

Available through the post or to download

The Weekend Card is all about continuity, assuring our clients of feedback on our selections – win or lose.

Past copies are available to view online or by calling us and requesting a **free information pack**.

5 Issues £30: 10 Issues £55: 20 Issues £100: 30 Issues £145

Tel: 01539 741 007

Email: rebecca@martenjulian.com

www.martenjulian.com

THE POINT-TO-POINT GRADUATES

JODIE STANDING

The point-to-point scene is an important nursery introduction for young horses and has paved the way for many of racing's biggest names including Best Mate, Denman, Native River and Samcro. The following 20 horses have each shown sufficient ability or potential to suggest they can make an impact under Rules for their new connections. As is the case with any horse they will thrive at different stages of their careers and it may take time before some of them fulfil their potential while others may be precocious enough to win bumpers and novice hurdles this season.

ANDY DUFRESNE (4YR BAY GELDING)

TRAINER:	**Gordon Elliott**
PEDIGREE:	**Doyen – Daytona Lily (Beneficial)**
FORM (P2P):	**1 -**
OPTIMUM TRIP:	**2m +**
GOING:	**Soft**

A very exciting top bumper prospect.

This son of Doyen made obvious appeal on his debut at Borris House and was sent off the 2/1 favourite under Jamie Codd for trainer Gordon Elliott in the colours of his travelling head girl Camilla Sharples.

Andy Dufresne could be seen travelling with effortless ease behind the strong pace before displaying a notable turn of foot going into the wings of the fourth from home. A slick leap at three out took him into a share of second position, but once Jamie Codd pressed the button and asked his mount to take charge, he did so in a matter of strides. A further injection of pace over the penultimate fence ensured a two-length lead quickly became five at the last where a super leap sent him soaring up the run-in to come home the eased down six-length winner.

Visually it was an impressive performance, backed up by the clock which recorded a time 16 seconds quicker than the day's average. The runner-up also looks smart and is highly thought of by Colin Tizzard, who paid a six-figure sum for him at the Aintree Sale in April.

Sharples, who has enjoyed many successful days on the track working for her boss, bought the horse as a three-year-old for €30,000 and garnered a healthy profit of £300,000 when the master of Cullentra House went to £330,000 to take him back home to race in the colours of J P McManus.

He is a half-brother to Clondaw Rigger, who won his point-to-point at Borris House before registering success under Rules. His dam Daytona Lily is a 2m hurdle winner and a sister to 3m hurdle/chase winner Its Crucial.

Described as very laid-back at home, Andy Dufresne is a very athletic, classy type with plenty of speed.

CHAMPAGNE PLATINUM (4YR GREY GELDING)

TRAINER:	**Nicky Henderson**
PEDIGREE:	**Stowaway – Saffron Holly (Roselier)**
FORM (P2P):	**1 -**
OPTIMUM TRIP:	**2m 4f +**
GOING:	**Soft**

One of only a handful to be sold for a six-figure sum at Aintree in April and will run in the colours of J P McManus.

The stoutly bred son of Stowaway made his debut only two weeks prior to the sale in a five-runner four-year-old maiden point-to-point at Quakerstown which only saw two competitors left to fight out the finish.

The game of cat and mouse began at the third from home where one of the three remaining horses took a tumble, leaving Champagne Platinum with the task of reeling in the heavily supported favourite who had made most of the running. He still had around three lengths to find on his rival jumping the penultimate fence, but responded well to his jockey's urgings on the downhill run to the last and began to close. An injection of speed from the grey around the home bend saw him poke his nose in front and he continued to pour on the pressure as they bypassed what would have been the final fence, eventually pulling six lengths clear at the line.

JP McManus – has acquired Andy Dufresne and Champagne Platinum

The runner-up was clearly highly thought of beforehand but could not sustain his effort at the business end of the race, and Champagne Platinum displayed a taking turn of foot and stamina to go by him on the run to the line without his rider ever resorting to the whip.

I liked what I saw in the paddock at Aintree and was not surprised to see him sell for £250,000. He's a fine big chasing sort with the scope to grow further. He understandably looked slightly on the weak side, but with a summer out at grass and plenty of time to fill his substantial frame, I would hope to see him develop into a nice sort this season.

A half-brother to The Chazer and Lismakeery, his dam is an unraced mare from the family of smart jumpers Saffron Lord and Gold Cup winner Saffron Tartan.

CHECKITOUT (4YR BAY GELDING)

TRAINER:	**Charlie Longsdon**
PEDIGREE:	**Salutino – Akasha (Stowaway)**
FORM (P2P):	**1 -**
OPTIMUM TRIP:	**2m 4f +**
GOING:	**Good to Soft**

A gorgeous looker who finished third in a hot maiden on his only start to date.

The appropriately named Checkitout lost nothing in defeat when coming home in third position behind the highly regarded The Very Man and Jasmin Des Bordes at Loughanmore, who fetched £210,000 and £145,000 respectively at the sales. With those prices, you'd have to think Charlie Longsdon has a bargain with this fellow at just £37,000.

The son of the relatively unknown German sire Salutino

Charlie Longsdon – has charge of Checkitout

jumped impeccably throughout the contest and saw a stride at the third from home which gained him a length or two in the air, causing him to touch down in front of the tightly grouped pack. He did his best to maintain his position after another good leap at the penultimate fence but couldn't match his rivals' turn of foot and was overtaken on the home bend. He stuck to his task in game fashion and ensured third position was in safekeeping following another spring-heeled leap at the last.

From the family of Black Op, Balthazar King, Agrapart and Afsoun, his dam is an unraced sister to three point-to-point winners.

Unfortunately, Checkitout has met with a setback and it is unlikely we'll see him before the new year, but nonetheless he is most definitely one to keep onside when he reaches the track.

He looked in tremendous spirits at his trainer's Open Day in the second week of September.

DEJA VUE (4YR BAY FILLY)

TRAINER:	**Anthony Honeyball**
PEDIGREE:	**Fame And Glory – Westgrove Berry (Presenting)**
FORM (P2P):	**1 -**
OPTIMUM TRIP:	**2m +**
GOING:	**Good to Soft**

An impeccably well-bred daughter of the late, great Fame And Glory whose stock have more than proved good value for money.

Deja Vue jumped with great aplomb from pillar to post and displayed a likeable attitude to dominate a modest point-to-point at Inch in late March under Richie Deegan. Never asked for maximum effort, the four-year-old began to turn the screw after the fourth from home and edged into a three-length advantage on the run to the third last. Brushing through the top of the birch did very little to interrupt the filly's momentum, and she pricked her ears when quickening on the approach to the penultimate fence. Another accomplished leap at the last allowed her to come home under hands and heels driving to record a comfortable four-length victory from Etincelle Lioterie who has subsequently been purchased by Margaret O'Toole for £50,000.

Anthony Honeyball does exceptionally well with the mares, with Ms Parfois, Midnight Tune, Cresswell Breeze, Duhallow Gesture and Tacenda just some of the names to have been successful for him last season.

Deja Vue is a half-sister to the decent hurdler and chaser, Jetstream Jack and is from the same family as Mendip Express and Grade 1 Feltham Novices' Chase winner Fiddling The Facts.

She will run in the colours of Axom Ltd and will be aimed at the Listed mares' bumper at the Cheltenham November meeting.

Anthony Honeyball – has some useful talent this season

DLAURO (5YR BAY GELDING)

TRAINER:	Joseph Patrick O'Brien
PEDIGREE:	Lauro – Gergovie De Bussy (Bad Conduct)
FORM (P2P):	1 -
OPTIMUM TRIP:	2m +
GOING:	Soft

A seriously impressive debutant winner with any amount of potential for races under Rules.

Dlauro could not have been more impressive when making all to win under Rob James on his debut at Belharbour, belying any understandable inexperience in the process.

The son of relatively new sire Lauro set the world alight from the front with some spectacular leaps reminiscent of a season-hardened chaser, not a newcomer to the scene. He never turned a hair throughout as he took the field along before a spectacular leap at the third from home eased the gelding into a three-length lead which readily became five lengths by the time they had reached the penultimate fence. James leisurely glanced over his shoulder as the pair went further clear on the long run to the last and jumped the fence in splendid isolation before coming home the heavily eased six-length winner from Seemingly So.

The form of the race received a significant boost in May when the third home, Alfie Corbitt, came out and won by 15 lengths and has subsequently been sold to Aiden Murphy for £68,000 to join Kim Bailey. The runner-up went to Olly Murphy for £100,000 and the fourth fell on his next start when still going well at the third from home.

Joseph O'Brien set the new record for a five-year-old point-to-point horse sold at public auction to the tune of £410,000 at the Tattersalls Ireland Sale at Cheltenham in February. He has been bought for Lloyd J Williams who has already formed a

Joseph O'Brien – quickly established himself as a top dual-purpose trainer

successful partnership with O'Brien on the Flat with victories in the Melbourne Cup with Rekindling and most recently the Irish Derby with Latrobe.

The five-year-old's pedigree is a blend of speed and stamina. His half-brother, Tepalo, won on the Flat in France up to 1m4f before being successful over hurdles over 3m. His dam was also a winner on the Flat in France over 1m7f.

Joseph O'Brien declared the five-year-old for a bumper at the Punchestown Festival earlier this year but withdrew him after he was discovered to be suffering from a temperature. The fact his handler was prepared to start him off in such a high-profile race indicates the high esteem in which he holds the gelding.

Dlauro looks destined for great things.

EDEN DU HOUX (4YR BAY GELDING)

TRAINER:	David Pipe
PEDIGREE:	Irish Wells – Maralypha (Louveteau)
FORM (P2P):	1 -
OPTIMUM TRIP:	2m +
GOING:	Soft

A very exciting recruit for David Pipe who will carry the colours of Professor Caroline Tisdall.

The four-year-old looked distinctly above average when he embarked on his debut in a well-contested maiden at

David Pipe – getting back on the map

Monksgrange in April. Harley Dunne struggled to settle his mount towards the rear of the field and made the decision to take much closer order at the fifth from home where the pair jumped into the lead.

The gelding settled much better at the head of affairs and was lightning quick over his next two fences on the uphill rise. Still cruising, he readily began to assert, lengthening his advantage on the turn for home and jumped the second last ears pricked before delivering a turn of foot on the run to the last. He spied the fence some way out and gave it a good look but jumped it perfectly before scooting up the run-in to win by an easy four lengths from the odds-on favourite and Denman relation, Tactical Move.

The clock was stopped with a time 10 seconds quicker than any other race on the day indicating it was a very decent contest. Given his exuberance in the early stages it is noteworthy how much he had left in the locker at the line. The son of Irish Wells also looked a real natural over his fences and has plenty of tactical speed to go with his turn of foot.

He is the first produce of an unraced half-sister to Lord Lyphard, a French 2m1f–2m5f hurdle winner, with the family linking back to an Italian 2m4f Grade 3 hurdle winner/2m5f French Listed winner.

David Pipe has trained some superstars over the years and has not had the ammunition in recent seasons, but this could be a horse to really put him back on the map. Tom Malone acquired the gelding in a private deal to run in the colours of Professor Caroline Tisdall who owns the likes of Mr Big Shot and Dell' Arca.

His previous handler at Baltimore Stables described him as a horse to definitely watch out for as they think he is quite special.

A very athletic sort, watch out for him making an impact in bumpers with Cheltenham most likely on the agenda.

ENERGUMENE (4YR BAY GELDING)

TRAINER:	Willie Mullins
PEDIGREE:	Denham Red – Olinight (April Night)
FORM (P2P):	1 -
OPTIMUM TRIP:	2m 4f +
GOING:	Soft

This British point winner was the subject of tremendous praise from his previous connections and could prove to be a special sort.

Energumene had always impressed in his work at home for his former handler Sophie Lacey before making his debut at Larkhill in January and was backed accordingly to go off the evens favourite for the first division of the open maiden race which saw a maximum field of 18 runners go to post.

Despite officially being only three and a half years old at the time of running, the son of Denham Red – the same sire as Un De Sceaux – showed no signs of inexperience and looked professional throughout. Tommie O'Brien kept a tight hold of him on the first circuit and anchored him towards the rear before making steady headway. He was quickly in contention and despite clouting the penultimate fence, the gelding found his stride and produced a good leap at the last, enabling him to touch down in front before quickening away on the tacky surface to win by two lengths.

Tom Lacey – husband of Sophie Lacey – said the horse is extremely impressive at home but was only half fit and expects there to be plenty more to come. In Lacey's words, this is a "very special horse" and added, "I think he's top drawer, I really do."

Given the high praise and the obvious links to the sire, it is of no surprise to see this promising sort join Willie Mullins. Blackbow, who was a favourite of mine, followed a similar route last term before landing a Grade 2 bumper at the inaugural Dublin Festival at Leopardstown for the Closutton handler but I'm led to believe that Energumene could be a good deal better.

This is one of the most exciting horses to look forward to and I expect him to be a leading bumper horse this term, with the Champion Bumper the ultimate target.

ENVOI ALLEN (4YR BAY GELDING)

TRAINER:	**Gordon Elliott**
PEDIGREE:	**Muhtathir – Reaction (Saint Des Saints)**
FORM (P2P):	**1 -**
OPTIMUM TRIP:	**2m +**
GOING:	**Good to Soft**

This could be a horse to reach the very top and his debut is eagerly anticipated.

Envoi Allen made his debut for Colin Bowe in the first four-year-old maiden of the 2018 season at Ballinaboola in February. In truth, he absolutely tanked his way throughout the race, never over-racing, but could easily have been called the winner some way from home.

He came up out of Barry O'Neill's hands at the fourth last but was restrained back on to the heels of the leader before rounding the bend for home. Many of his rivals were feeling the pinch on the soft ground coming down to three out, but Envoi Allen approached the fence at nothing more than a hack canter and breezed past the long-time leader upon touching down, once allowed an inch of rein. He continued to pull further clear on the run to the last under his motionless rider and, ears pricked, he jumped the fence before displaying an electric turn of foot to power through the line to record a widening 10-length success.

Ballinaboola point-to-point course

Despite not jumping the last three fences with the greatest of conviction, there were no signs of the engine stalling and the manner in which he travelled before quickening really was a sight to behold. The form also looks strong with the third, Danny Kirwan's half-brother, Appreciate It, going on to win on his next start and the fourth home placing twice since.

Being a first foal, he is a very powerful unit with a great amount of presence. Not massive – but extremely well built – there's a great deal of quality to him.

His dam is a dual 2m7f cross-country winner in France. She is a half-sister to Auvergnat and French 2m5f Grade 3 winner Une Epoque from the family of Gavin Cromwell's smart juvenile hurdle winner Espoir D'Allen.

Given the impression he created between the flags, it was no surprise to see him pass through the sales ring for £400,000 at

Cheltenham in February, going the way of Tom Malone. He will now race in the colours of David and Patricia Thompson of Cheveley Park Stud for trainer Gordon Elliott.

This really is a classy individual with speed to match his stamina.

FAITHFULNESS (5YR BAY MARE)

TRAINER:	**Charlie Longsdon**
PEDIGREE:	**Robin Des Champs – Ballycowan Lady (Accordion)**
FORM (P2P):	**1**
OPTIMUM TRIP:	**2m 4f +**
GOING:	**Soft**

One for the decent mares' races this season.

Faithfulness looked a useful sort when winning in convincing style on her debut in a five-year-old mares' maiden at Monksgrange at the end of April. She travelled powerfully throughout the race in mid-division but jumped herself into a closer position at the fifth from home. A bold leap over the fourth last stole her a length or two in the air and she readily began to eat up the ground on the climb to three out. She soon progressed to the lead on the landing side and came to the penultimate fence with a two-length lead which quickly became eight lengths at the last which she maintained to the line.

This scopey daughter of Robin Des Champs really knows how to jump and she appeared to relish the testing ground conditions.

A full sister to bumper winner and useful hurdler Duke Des Champs, her dam is an unraced half-sister to high-class staying chaser Harbour Pilot, with the further family stretching back to Monty's Pass.

She's not devoid of speed but, already a five-year-old, I would imagine Charlie Longsdon will be starting her off over hurdles and she should come into her own over middle distances.

FEEL MY PULSE (4YR BAY GELDING)

TRAINER:	**Gordon Elliott**
PEDIGREE:	**Stowaway – Zenaide (Zaffaran)**
FORM (P2P):	**1 -**
OPTIMUM TRIP:	**2m 4f +**
GOING:	**Soft**

Feel My Pulse has to be up there as one of the most exciting horses to look forward to this coming season.

The stoutly bred son of Stowaway commanded a serious amount of respect in the ring at the Cheltenham Festival Sale in March following a hugely impressive front-running display just five days earlier on his debut in a four-year-old maiden at Lismore.

The four-year-old was booted to the front by Rob James as the flag went up and they didn't see another rival as the gelding produced an exhibition round of jumping and a ground-eating stride on the way to annihilating the five-runner field in testing conditions.

Feel My Pulse really began to motor once jumping the fourth from home and, despite the runner-up closing for a stride or two on the approach to the penultimate fence, he was no match for the gelding who kicked on once again when given an inch of rein from the motionless Rob James.

Still hard on the bridle rounding the bend for home, he winged the final fence and went through the line powerfully.

Some of the most prolific National Hunt horses have made

their debuts at this track with the likes of Best Mate and Florida Pearl chief amongst them. I'm not saying this fellow can turn out to be as good as them, but he couldn't have started off better.

A half-brother to Listed hurdle winner Myska, useful bumper winner Daring Carlotta and point/hurdle winner Six Gun Serenade, his dam was a useful bumper performer and a half-sister to hurdle/chase winner up to 3m Very Stylish.

Margaret O'Toole, who buys the majority of the Gigginstown House Stud horses, went to a top lot-equalling sum of £330,000 to secure the gelding who now enters training with Gordon Elliott.

Still a very unfurnished model, he could turn into a decent bumper type, but it is unlikely we'll see his true ability until much further down the line when sent over fences.

FINANCIER (5YR CHESTNUT GELDING)

TRAINER:	Kerry Lee
PEDIGREE:	Dubawi – Desired (Rainbow Quest)
FORM (P2P):	1
OPTIMUM TRIP:	2m +
GOING:	Good to Soft

An exciting prospect with one of the best pedigrees in the book.

The money came for Financier when he landed the odds in impressive fashion at Witton Castle in early May.

The well-bred gelding dwarfed his opposition in the Open Maiden as he travelled powerfully on the pace to jump the fourth from home in a share of the lead before being left out in front at the next when a horse went through the wings of the fence. Rounding the turn for home he was still hard on the steel but had to dodge a loose horse as it went across him on the approach to the penultimate fence. Once straightened up he popped over nicely and quickened impressively on the approach to the last where he produced an almighty leap which saw him gain a length in the air before sprinting to the finish to record an impressive two-and-a-half-length victory under Jack Teal.

Bought for £16,000 when offered by Sheikh Mohammed's Godolphin operation in January 2016 by Nicky Tinkler, he returned to Doncaster in May following his victory and was purchased by Kerry Lee for £115,000.

Kerry Lee's father, Richard, said the son of Dubawi was "the one horse they really wanted at the sale" and described him as having "very decent bone" and likened him to stable stalwart Top Gamble.

Kerry Lee – building up her young stock

As you would expect from his pedigree he is related to a number of talented performers from the Flat including half-brothers Desideratum, a French 1m4f Group 3 winner, and Poet Laureate, a French 12.5f Listed winner. His dam is an unraced half-sister to Racing Post Trophy winner Medaaly and high-class 7f–1m colt Charnwood Forest.

Richard Lee felt he may take in a bumper before sending him straight into the novice chase division, but it would all depend on his work at home.

INTERCONNECTED (4YR BROWN GELDING)

TRAINER:	Nicky Henderson
PEDIGREE:	Network – R De Rien Sivola (Robin Des Champs)
FORM:	F1 -
OPTIMUM TRIP:	2m 4f +
GOING:	Good/Soft

This is a real chasing sort for the future.

The ex-Tom-Lacey-owned gelding set a record figure for a British point-to-point graduate sold at public auction when going the way of Anthony Bromley of Highflyer Bloodstock for £220,000 at the Tattersalls Cheltenham Sale in March.

The son of Network – sire of Sprinter Sacre – fell on his debut at Thorpe Lodge in January when still travelling smoothly but atoned for his mistake next time at Larkhill in February when coming home head-in-chest to win by 20 lengths. He jumped and travelled with effortless ease on the heels of the leaders throughout the three-mile contest and came clear as he liked after the third from home.

He's a big, burly horse but very light on his feet for his size and although he showed no signs of not enjoying the good ground at Larkhill, his knee action may suggest a softer surface could also suit.

Out of R De Rien Sivola, who was Grade 2 placed over hurdles, this is only her second foal with his half-sister Little Miss Poet already a winner for Philip Hobbs.

Trainer Sophie Lacey brought Blackbow through the British pointing ranks last season before selling him to Willie Mullins, and this looks another which will make into a fine performer on the track, going the way of Nicky Henderson for owners Mike Grech and Stuart Parkin.

KING ROLAND (4YR BROWN GELDING)

TRAINER:	**Harry Fry**
PEDIGREE:	**Stowaway – Kiltiernan Robin (Robin Des Champs)**
FORM (P2P):	**1 -**
OPTIMUM TRIP:	**2m 4f +**
GOING:	**Good to Soft**

King Roland treated the racegoers at Larkhill to an exhibition-like performance on Easter Saturday when thrashing his opposition by an easy 10 lengths.

Confidence was obviously high as the Sophie Lacey-trained newcomer was well supported and went off the evens favourite despite a well-regarded Richard Kelvin-Hughes-owned debutant also in the line-up. Never too far off the pace, the eye couldn't help but be drawn to the scopey son of Stowaway who always travelled well under Tommie O'Brien. A bad blunder from his chief market rival at the third from home allowed the gelding to ease into a healthy lead which he continued to extend as he devoured up the ground on the run to the line, and he finished 10 lengths clear of Imogens Thunder with a further five lengths back to Foxworthy, who is now with Nicky Henderson.

With so much left in the tank, Tommie O'Brien struggled to pull up the four-year-old and had to travel a further three furlongs before eventually coming to a stop. Following the race, O'Brien described the performance as exceptional, and as good a debut as he has seen in 10 years of point-to-pointing.

He's a typical lanky Stowaway gelding with a large frame to fill, so he is obviously going to get stronger as he matures. Most of the sire's stock perform well on a testing surface but this one showed good pace on the good ground and may have enough speed for a bumper.

Harry Fry has secured the exciting prospect in a private deal and he will run in the colours of Masterson Holdings, who own horses such as Fletchers Flyer and Minella Awards with the Dorset trainer.

QUOI DE NEUF (4YR BAY GELDING)

TRAINER:	Evan Williams
PEDIGREE:	Anzillero – Qualite Controlee (Poliglote)
FORM (P2P):	1 -
OPTIMUM TRIP:	2m +
GOING:	Soft

Here is an easy winner of a maiden point-to-point at Ballysteen in April – a race previously won by the mighty Faugheen.

The son of Anzillero was ridden with patience under Derek O'Connor at the rear of the field but gradually moved closer towards the fourth last and showed good speed to take second position on the run to the next. Despite taking the fence by the roots he quickly regathered his stride after a few kicks in the belly and went into a clear lead before the penultimate fence and lengthened his advantage further on the downhill run to the last. A brilliant leap there highlighted how much energy was left in the tank as he went on to win by an easy nine lengths from Howling Milan, who was subsequently disqualified after winning on his next start.

This looked an above-average maiden and was run in the fastest time of the day.

Evan Williams has paid big money for point-to-point recruits over the years and Quoi De Neuf, who cost €180,000, looks another decent acquisition and has the potential to reach a good level.

A half-brother to 2015 Fred Winter Juvenile Hurdle winner Qualando and the Willie Mullins-trained Au Quart De Tour, his dam was a winner on the Flat before being successful over hurdles and fences.

He should have plenty of speed to be competitive in bumpers and looks to possess the ability necessary to develop into a nice type.

SHADOW RIDER (4YR CHESTNUT GELDING)

TRAINER:	**TBC**
PEDIGREE:	**Martaline – Samansonnienne (Mansonnien)**
FORM (P2P):	**1 -**
OPTIMUM TRIP:	**2m +**
GOING:	**Soft/Heavy**

This well-related son of Martaline announced himself on to the pointing scene with an impressive victory at Knockanard in a

2m4f contest in February and left the impression he could be a very special individual.

Shadow Rider tracked the leaders moving well before making a more serious challenge at the fourth from home where a slight mistake did very little to alter his momentum. He still only appeared to be in second gear as the pack climbed the steep uphill rise and jumped the next two fences with great accuracy before reeling in the long-time leader on the brow of the hill. Now in a one-length lead but still not asked for an effort he popped over the last before impressively pulling clear with his ground-eating stride and crossed the line powerfully to win by a widening six lengths.

This was a serious performance in the testing conditions, highlighting the engine size of the gelding. The effortlessness with which he climbed the hill before finding an extra gear once jumping the final fence left the impression he was just warming up.

From a useful family including being a full brother to Gordon Elliott's useful 2m–2m5f hurdler Squouateur, his half-brothers include 2m4f–3m1f hurdle winner and useful chaser Samingarry and French 2m3f hurdle winner Sarabas. His dam is a French 2m1f–2m2f hurdle and later chase winner.

The ground the gelding is able to cover with his powerful stride could be a serious weapon under Rules and may be seen to best effect on a testing surface. At four years of age, turning five in January, he may go straight over obstacles but ultimately his future lies over fences when covering a distance of ground.

SOLDIER AT WAR (4YR BAY GELDING)

TRAINER:	**Gordon Elliott**
PEDIGREE:	**Soldier Hollow – Sang Sun (Monsun)**
FORM (P2P):	**2 -**
OPTIMUM TRIP:	**2m +**
GOING:	**Soft**

Soldier At War lost nothing in defeat when coming home in second behind Malone Road on his only start to date.

The son of Soldier Hollow travelled powerfully at the head of the field from the drop of the flag and was still well in command after the third from home. He had all bar the favourite beaten off on the turn into the home straight and although another sound leap at the penultimate fence helped him gain momentum, Malone Road began to mount his challenge. They locked horns over the final fence and although this gelding was brave and battled all the way to the line, he didn't have the staying power and was outpointed towards the finish.

This was a very encouraging effort and leaves the impression that he'll have a fruitful career under Rules. Gordon Elliott, who was alongside Tom Malone when buying the favourite for a sales-topping figure of £325,000 at Aintree in April, also took home this gelding for less than half that price at £140,000 – teaming up with Aiden O'Ryan.

Soldier At War is a half-brother to Sang Tiger, a French/Irish Flat winner and later Irish hurdle winner, and Sang Dasher, a French 2m hurdle winner and Belgian Flat winner. The dam was also a German 6f Flat winner and later a jumps winner.

Given the speed-biased pedigree the gelding did well to show so much over three miles and should progress into a decent bumper performer at the big tracks this term.

THATSY (4YR BAY GELDING)

TRAINER:	Gordon Elliott
PEDIGREE:	Martaline – Rainallday (Cadoudal)
FORM (P2P):	12 -
OPTIMUM TRIP:	2m +
GOING:	Good to Soft

This is a really likeable gelding with plenty of potential for a top stable.

Thatsy made all to win by an easy three lengths on his debut at Lingstown in March under a confident ride from James Walsh. The son of Martaline was ponderous and sticky at a few of his fences – notably the last two – but he has a lovely long, lolloping stride and also the ability to quicken, as he demonstrated when putting distance between himself and the rest of the field in the latter stages.

On his second start, just under three weeks later, he lost nothing in defeat when finishing second, beaten a head by the far more experienced Manetti at Loughanmore. The form of the race looks strong, with the winner going on to win by 30 lengths on his next start and the third home winning a hunter chase very easily by the same distance for Peter Maher.

Always up with the pace in the five-runner event, Thatsy stalked the eventual winner until a tremendous jump took him to the front at the third from home. A quicker leap from Manetti at the next saw them lock horns turning for home and a tough tussle up the home straight, once jumping the last together, saw experience rise to the fore.

This was a game performance for only a four-year-old who is sizeable in stature. He may take time to fully mature and fill out his frame and may be seen to even greater effect on some decent ground, although soft ground has posed no problems so far.

A half-brother to a hurdle winner over 2m in France, his dam was placed over hurdles and is a half-sister to a 1m2f performer on the Flat, with the family linking back to French Oaks third Raintree Renegade.

He is one to note in bumpers this season and it may not be long before he starts repaying some of the £130,000 which he cost at Cheltenham in April.

Although officially described as being a bay, you'll notice when he hits the track that he is very much a grey gelding.

THE HOLLOW CHAP (4YR CHESTNUT GELDING)

TRAINER:	Rose Dobbin
PEDIGREE:	Beat Hollow – An Banog (Anshan)
FORM (P2P):	1 -
OPTIMUM TRIP:	2m +
GOING:	Good to Soft

This is a well-bred son of Beat Hollow who should make an impact for his northern yard.

The Hollow Chap – a half-brother to the talented but mercurial Arkle winner Western Warhorse – displayed plenty of pace on his debut in a four-year-old maiden at Tinahely in February when taking the field along in a share of the lead for a decent part of the contest. He was lucky to survive a shuddering blunder at the third from home which had his rider at the buckle end momentarily, but they soon picked up and resumed their prominent position before jumping the next more fluently.

The pace notably increased on the run to the final fence and although challenged, he responded gamely and lengthened into the wings of the fence before producing a big leap which helped him to surge up the run-in and win going away, recording a time 10 seconds quicker than the day's average.

Beyondapproach, who fought tenaciously towards the finish, confirmed the form when winning on her next start by two lengths and the fourth home also subsequently finished runner-up on his next start in a very decent maiden won by Ask For Glory.

Gerry Hogan, buying on behalf of Rose Dobbin, went to £140,000 at the Cheltenham Festival Sale in March and the trainer reports that the gelding has done well over the summer.

He will most likely be starting off his career in a bumper in the north, possibly at Kelso or Carlisle this winter.

TIPPINGITUPTONANCY (4YR CHESTNUT FILLY)

TRAINER:	Tim Vaughan
PEDIGREE:	Stowaway – Dyrick Daybreak (Ali-Royal)
FORM (P2P):	2 -
OPTIMUM TRIP:	2m 4f +
GOING:	Good to Soft

This tough and strong daughter of Stowaway comes from the handler responsible for last year's Supreme Novices' Hurdle winner Summerville Boy and also star performers The Tullow Tank, Standing Ovation and Seeyouatmidnight.

Tippingituptonancy created a lasting impression when filling the runners-up spot at Horse and Jockey in an ultra-competitive mares' maiden in March this year.

The good-looking four-year-old attacked her fences with confidence at the head of affairs and took the field along at a decent pace. Overtaken at the penultimate fence by Little Light and The Glancing Queen, she could quite easily have folded and

Stowaway – sire of the highly promising King Roland and Tippingituptonancy

given up the fight, but to her credit she rose to the challenge and fought back bravely on the inside to press for second jumping the last. She flew over the fence as her rival took a fall and stayed on strongly to press the eventual winner all the way up the run-in, only to be denied by a diminishing three-quarters of a length.

This looked a decent race, backed up by the time which was recorded as the second quickest on the day. The winner, The Glancing Queen, has since been purchased by Alan King for £80,000 whilst the unlucky faller Little Light went through the ring to Aiden Murphy for £200,000 and will run in the colours of J P Magnier.

Tippingituptonancy was expensive at £185,000 but she looks a decent purchase for Tim Vaughan and I am sure he will be placing her to good effect.

A half-sister to the highly regarded Grade 2 winner Mr Whipped, out of the talented Grade 2-winning mare Dyrick Daybreak, I feel she may be a surprise package and is one I'm very much looking forward to this season.

YOUNG BULL (4YR BAY GELDING)

TRAINER:	**Harry Whittington**
PEDIGREE:	**Dubai Destination – Jane Hall (Saddlers' Hall)**
FORM (P2P):	**2F -**
OPTIMUM TRIP:	**2m 4f +**
GOING:	**Soft**

Young Bull could be one to slip under the radar.

The four-year-old has shown plenty of potential on both starts despite not getting his head in front. He finished 15 lengths behind his talented stable companion Feel My Pulse on his debut at Lismore in March. Despite being outclassed by his rival – who went on to fetch £330,000 at the sales – he travelled strongly throughout and was still clinging on to the coat-tails at the third from home before being steadily outpaced.

Harry Whittington – has the promising Young Bull

On his second start at Durrow he was in the midst of a good run when tipping up at the fourth from home, having set a good pace up until that point.

From the evidence I have seen so far, I think Young Bull is a progressive four-year-old who can go well for his new connections.

Harry Whittington had the eye to pick up Court Liability after he finished placed on his point-to-point debut and he is now unbeaten in three starts under Rules.

Young Bull is a half-brother to useful performer Shanroe Santos, City Break and also Seemingly So. His dam is an unraced half-sister to useful bumper and chase winners Boca Boca and Precarium.

He will probably go straight over hurdles and there could be plenty of fun to be had with him.

Marten's Latest News

If you want to keep in touch with Marten's latest thoughts ring him on:

0906 150 1555

Selections given in the first minute

Calls charged at £1.50 a minute at all times & your telecom provider will add their own Access Charge. Please contact your provider for their charges.

Telephone & Text Service

A non-premium rate version of this line is available. Please call the office if you'd like to join or order online. The line is an 03 number which is the same as calling a landline and included in a mobile phone package. Marten sends a text message direct each day. Prices also available online.

TAKING A LOOK BACK

JODIE STANDING

My point-to-point feature in last year's *Dark Horses Jumps Guide* was the biggest to date and it helped to shine the light on many bright young prospects, some of which ended up winning at the highest level.

Of those horses mentioned, the Nicky Henderson-trained duo **Santini** and On the Blind Side fared best, with the former rounding off a successful novice hurdle campaign with a Grade 1 victory in the Doom Bar Sefton Novices' Hurdle at Aintree in April.

Prior to that he notched up back-to-back victories starting at Newbury on his debut before winning a Grade 2 at Cheltenham where he beat subsequent Grade 1 winner Black Op. He then went on to finish a never-nearer third in the Albert Bartlett Novices' Hurdle at the Cheltenham Festival on his first attempt at three miles.

With the scope to develop mentally and physically, Santini could be a leading novice chaser this term and although the RSA over 3m½f looks the obvious place to aim, the JLT Novices' Chase could be the preferred option for which he is 25/1.

On The Blind Side proved to be a tough and consistent performer, winning in gritty style on his debut at Aintree before staying on strongly at Cheltenham and impressing at Sandown, both in Grade 2 company.

He was reported to be sore behind on the lead up to the Cheltenham Festival which caused him to miss the meeting, but he pitched up at Aintree in the Grade 1 Mersey Novices' Hurdle only to finish sixth behind Black Op. He's an embryonic chaser and an exciting horse to look forward to this season over

Ian Williams – now has charge of Cracking Destiny

fences. He will start off over 2m4f but will excel at staying trips with the RSA Novices' Chase possibly the ultimate target, for which he is currently 20/1.

Henderson also has **Kupatana**, who appeared to relish a trip and is capable of winning again from her current hurdles mark of 122, while **Indian Hawk** looks more at home over fences but needs top of the ground. **Cracking Destiny** was very backward and weak last term and has since switched yards to Ian Williams. The five-year-old has been doing plenty of work over the summer to strengthen him up and he remains with potential.

Willie Mullins' bumper horses performed well, and my favourite, **Blackbow**, landed the Grade 2 Goffs Future Stars event at the inaugural Dublin Racing Festival at Leopardstown. He then stayed on at the one pace to be fifth in the Champion Bumper before rounding off his solid campaign with a fine effort to be second at Punchestown behind Tornado Flyer. He'll be seen in a much better light this term once covering a distance of ground over hurdles and looks tailor-made for the Albert Bartlett.

Carefully Selected was another to impress.

He made a winning debut in a 2m4f bumper at Leopardstown before dropping back in distance to make all at Naas. He employed the same tactics in the Champion Bumper at Cheltenham and led everywhere but the line before finishing third behind Tornado Flyer and Blackbow at Punchestown. He is another who will benefit from a distance of ground and could be aimed at the top staying novices.

Dorrells Pierji was on the 'Five to Follow' list after an emphatic point-to-point win but disappointed on his first two bumper starts last spring before landing the odds at Wexford in a minor event when stepped up in trip to 2m4f.

He confirmed that was no fluke at Galway over two miles and latterly impressed in a 2m4f maiden hurdle at Listowel which he won by 14 lengths with a further 12 lengths back to the third. That was on soft ground which bodes well if connections keep him going through the winter months.

Blackbow – expected to reach the top over hurdles

Another gelding which looked well above average last season and could develop into a top-quality novice hurdler is **Brewin'Upastorm**.

The five-year-old impressed on his debut at Hereford to beat Grade 2 Aintree bumper winner Portrush Ted which earned high praise from his trainer Olly Murphy who said, "He's the best in the yard."

He then ran a solid race on unsuitably soft ground at Newbury in a Listed contest where his effort petered out up the home straight after making up plenty of ground from the rear of the field. He is likely to start off at a low level but he's an exciting prospect and hopes are high that he can fulfil his promise.

The Paul Nicholls-trained **Posh Trish** is a strong mare and could flourish over obstacles this term after starting off so well last season, notching up back-to-back victories – once at Listed level – before finding the boys too strong for her at Ascot in a very well-contested bumper. She fared better back against her own sex at Sandown and she should come into her own over hurdles.

The Dellercheckout and **Some Man** are also worth noting this season. They were both weak, backward types last term and although the latter did run well on his debut, they both struggled and should make more of an impact this term with another summer under their belts.

Global Citizen started his career for Jonjo O'Neill but after winning on his bumper debut he failed to fire and appeared to struggle to see out his races on his next two starts over hurdles.

A switch to Ben Pauling's stable brought about improvement and he impressed when beating subsequent smart hurdler Euxton Lane by eight lengths at Southwell before stepping up in grade to land the Dovecote Hurdle at Kempton in style. He was slightly disappointing at Aintree but it later transpired he pulled his muscles in the bottomless conditions.

Global Citizen – possible Champion Hurdle contender

The six-year-old will stay hurdling this term and it's not out of the question that he may be aimed at the Champion Hurdle for which he is a 33/1 shot. He's very slick over his obstacles but needs good ground.

Court Liability was the model of consistency for Harry Whittington and notched up the hat-trick under a penalty at Hereford in November having won on his bumper debut at Fontwell in October and a novices' hurdle at Sedgefield in early November.

Unfortunately his season came to a premature end after a suspensory sprain sidelined him, but he's done well over the summer and will remain over hurdles. The plan is to get him qualified for the Pertemps Final at the Cheltenham Festival in March.

Nigel Twiston-Davies made an early start with **Ballymoy** and he ran well, despite being keen, to finish third to Simply The Betts in a bumper at Market Rasen before running an OK sort of race to finish fifth behind Kalashnikov in November in a maiden hurdle.

Wind surgery appeared to do wonders for the gelding on his reappearance in February as he won comfortably by seven lengths at Uttoxeter and proved that was no fluke next time at Bangor when running away to a 21-length success. He rounded off a solid second half of the season by winning the valuable bet365 Novices' Hurdle at Sandown and is now rated on a mark of 139.

He looks one of Nigel Twiston-Davies' nicer novices and may be sent chasing sooner rather than later.

Evan Williams' **Chooseyourweapon** is a staying chaser for the future but fared well last term over hurdles and won back-to-back races at Chepstow before finding a step up in company to Grade 2 level a bridge too far. He then disappointed down in a lesser event on a return to Chepstow but with a summer under his belt he can resume his winning ways this season. He's not blessed with a tremendous amount of gears, but he stays well and loves the mud.

By his own high standards Jonjo O'Neill endured a torrid season and his expensive purchase **Palmers Hill** ultimately disappointed after showing good promise to win over two miles on his hurdles debut at Uttoxeter.

He was then well supported at Ascot on his next start but appeared to not get home over the 2m5½f trip and ran a similar sort of race on soft ground at Sandown over 2m4f on his final start. His breeding suggests he should stay and a rating of 124 looks extremely workable given the ability and level of form he showed in his point-to-points.

Slate House beat Supreme Novices' Hurdle winner Summerville Boy in a Grade 2 at Cheltenham in November having won a maiden at the track the previous month. He then became disappointing, perhaps attributable to the soft and heavy ground, but did hint at a return to form in the Grade 1 Supreme Novices' until taking a heavy fall at the last. He looks the type that Colin Tizzard does well with over fences.

Storm Home was holding Getabird at bay when he fell in his point-to-point but has so far not lived up to expectations despite winning twice over obstacles. He remains unexposed over 2m4f–3m and could benefit for a step up in trip.

Alan King's **Good Man Pat** appeared to be holding a bit back for himself but improved for a step up to three miles in ordinary company before finding Grade 1 level a step too far at Aintree. He may struggle from a mark of 135 over hurdles and could benefit from going novice chasing.

By contrast Kerry Lee's gelding **Kings Monarch** looks leniently treated on a mark of 116 and could be one to keep a close eye on when stepped up in trip in a handicap.

He has been staying on from off the pace over inadequate distances and looks an improver.

Lee also has **Storm Control** on a feasible mark of 127. He's a horse I have a lot of time for and features in my 'Ten to Follow'.

He showed a decent level of ability in some hot races last term and was pencilled in for a Grade 1 contest in January. He'll be seen in a better light over fences, but is also capable of landing a handicap hurdle over a trip in excess of 2m4f.

Another to keep an eye on in the handicap hurdle department is Oliver Sherwood's **Pontresina**. He found himself completely stuck in the mud on his first two starts under Rules but fared much better on good ground in the spring, Rated on a mark of 117, he should be competitive when conditions are to suit.

More can also be expected from Dan Skelton's mare **Maire Banrigh** who benefited from a wind surgery procedure to win on her third start over hurdles after failing to get home on her first two attempts. She's a strong traveller and looks underrated on a mark of 112. Good ground over 2m–2m4f could be ideal.

Tom George's **Net De Treve** ran well in a decent bumper at Doncaster on his debut before lacking the pace to get competitive at Exeter in May. It was a similar tale of events for

Dan Skelton – can have a good season with Maire Banrigh

Rose Dobbin's **Hitman Fred**, who showed good promise to finish second at Kelso on his debut before disappointing on a revisit to the track in February. By Getaway out of an Oscar mare, he is bred to relish a trip with the emphasis on stamina.

Over in Ireland, Jessica Harrington's duo **Madison To Monroe** and **Moonshine Bay** have yet to shine despite both winning moderate events. The former appreciated the step up to three miles at Tipperary in May as did the latter who will now go chasing, which he is bred for.

Heroesandvillains will relish staying distances once tackling fences, while **Stay Humble** has started to show a decent level of ability having encountered some better ground during the summer months. He was very impressive at Sligo on his latest start.

Battleoverdoyen, **Cool Getaway**, **Copper Gone West**, **Monbeg Zena**, **Mr Lingo** and **Sending Love** have yet to appear for their new connections.

THE TEN TO FOLLOW

JODIE STANDING

I have selected the following horses for this special list as they have either impressed me with their physical appearance, their performance, their potential or all three. Some are more obvious than others, but I believe they will all be successful and yield a profit this season.

BLACK OP (7YR BROWN GELDING)

TRAINER:	**Tom George**
PEDIGREE:	**Sandmason – Afar Story (Desert Story)**
FORM (P2P):	**1/**
FORM (BUMPER):	**19/**
FORM (HURDLES):	**41221 -**
OPTIMUM TRIP:	**2m 4f +**
GOING:	**Soft**
HURDLES RATING:	**152**

Black Op came of age last season and looks an exciting prospect for the novice chasing division this term.

Tom George's stable star won his only point-to-point and made an instant impression in the bumper sphere back in February 2017 when beating subsequent smart hurdler Claimantakinforgan by a widening two and a half lengths. He then failed to fire when stepped up in company to compete in the Grade 2 Aintree bumper and trailed home in ninth position.

The son of Sandmason returned to action in a 2m½f National Hunt maiden hurdle at Newbury in December 2017 and finished fourth to Lostintranslation, where he travelled well but made mistakes. He relished the step up to 2m5f on his next start at Doncaster and made all before powering clear of Colonial Dreams to win by 17 lengths.

He then took a step up in company for the Grade 2 Ballymore Classic Novices' Hurdle at Cheltenham in late January and went to the front some way from home. He looked the likely winner coming to the last, but a terrible mistake allowed Santini to take aim and slipstream him on the run to the line.

Black Op returned to Cheltenham to contest the Grade 1 Ballymore Novices' Hurdle at the Cheltenham Festival and took the eye in a major way in the preliminaries. He looked exceptional and ran accordingly, only finding Samcro two and

Black Op – a fine strapping sort for chasing

three quarter lengths too good for him. He was never going to beat the winner, but he stayed on gamely and kept Gordon Elliott's charge honest all the way to the line.

The seven-year-old rounded off a superb season with a deserved Grade 1 success in the Betway Mersey Novices' Hurdle at Aintree's Grand National meeting. Again, as he had done previously, he took up the running some way from home but made a hash of the third last and looked in trouble when headed by Western Ryder and Momella at the penultimate flight. Another unconvincing leap at the last did nothing to aid his cause and allowed old rival Lostintranslation to take over only for Black Op to renew his effort and regain the upper hand in the gamest fashion close home.

Black Op is a big strapping horse and will be sent novice chasing this term. It's a strong division, but his courage and effectiveness on deep ground will stand strong in his favour.

BREWIN'UPASTORM (5YR BAY GELDING)

TRAINER:	**Olly Murphy**
PEDIGREE:	**Milan – Daraheen Diamond (Husyan)**
FORM (P2P):	**1/**
FORM (BUMPER):	**14 -**
OPTIMUM TRIP:	**2m +**
GOING:	**Good to Soft**

Brewin'Upastorm created a lasting impression, despite being given a light campaign last season, and could be the type to really come into his own over obstacles.

The five-year-old was an eight-length winner of a point-to-point at Quakerstown when trained by Tim Hyde in Ireland and was snapped up by Ryan Mahon for £250,000. Originally sent to be trained by Dan Skelton, he was moved to Olly Murphy's yard before his Rules debut.

The son of Milan was unleashed in a bumper at Hereford in January and came home an impressive nine-length winner under Fergus Gregory. He took a wide path throughout, possibly in search of better ground, and powered to the front two furlongs from home before stretching right away from Portrush Ted, who has subsequently won the Grade 2 bumper at Aintree's Grand National meeting. The third home, Blue Flight, has also come out and won.

He then ran a solid race in a Listed bumper on unsuitably soft ground at Newbury's Betfair Hurdle meeting. Anchored towards the rear of the field, he started to make a move down the side of the course and although he managed to travel into a prominent position up the home straight, his effort petered out in the final furlong and he settled for fourth place behind Acey Milan, who went on to finish fourth in the Champion Bumper at the Cheltenham Festival.

Brewin'Upastorm has been trained very much with the future in mind and will probably start at a low level over hurdles before progressing through the ranks as the season develops. He was a good jumper of a fence in his point-to-point days, which bodes well for him taking to hurdles, and although he has plenty of pace and a turn of foot, his pedigree suggests he may benefit from a step up in trip to 2m4f.

DUHALLOW GESTURE (6YR BAY MARE)

TRAINER:	**Anthony Honeyball**
PEDIGREE:	**King's Theatre – Rare Gesture (Shalford)**
FORM (P2P):	**P1 -**
FORM (BUMPER):	**00/113**
OPTIMUM TRIP:	**2m +**
GOING:	**Good to Soft**

Anthony Honeyball has done very well with mares and Duhallow Gesture looks like she could follow the trend this season as she embarks on a campaign over obstacles.

The daughter of King's Theatre failed to fire in two bumpers early in her career before switching to the pointing field where she was disappointing on her first start before winning at Quakerstown in April 2017. She then went on to win a 2m2f bumper at Tipperary for her handler Damian Murphy before joining her current connections after going through the ring for £100,000.

After a few training issues she made her stable debut on Boxing Day and rewarded her new owner's patience to win the Listed bumper at Huntingdon, where she produced a good turn of foot before signs of greenness to beat Diamond Gait by a little over two lengths. She then went on to finish a gallant third in the Grade 2 mares' bumper at Aintree's Grand National meeting where she attempted to make all under Richie McLernon only to be collared deep inside the final furlong.

The jockey was extremely positive in the post-race debrief and said she wasn't stopping towards the finish but the others quickened passed her. The plan this season is to have a campaign aiming at the Mares' Novices' Hurdle at the Cheltenham Festival in March.

This is a lovely well-put-together mare with an athletic step and a relaxed nature, but most importantly she is very genuine with a good blend of speed and stamina. Given that she has won a bumper over 2m2f and comes from the family of Rhinestone Cowboy and Wichita Lineman, there should be no problem with staying intermediate distances and even further.

Most definitely a name for anyone's shortlist this season.

The gathering mist

JARVEYS PLATE (5YR CHESTNUT GELDING)

Trainer:	Fergal O'Brien
PEDIGREE:	Getaway – She's Got To Go (Glacial Storm)
FORM (P2P):	23 -
FORM (BUMPER):	1 -
OPTIMUM TRIP:	2m 4f +
GOING:	Soft

Fergal O'Brien's yard enjoyed a tremendous season last term, not least with Poetic Rhythm, but also his other bumper runners and Jarveys Plate looks one of the nicer ones to rise through the ranks.

The stoutly bred son of Getaway started his career in the Irish point-to-point field and was placed twice, the first of which has worked out well with the winner, Court Master finding only the smart James Ewart-trained Black Pirate too good for him on his Rules debut. Following the good run, Fergal purchased the gelding privately to run in 'The Yes No Wait Sorries' colours.

Fairly late to the scene, he made his Rules debut towards the end of April in a well-contested bumper at Perth and was well supported to go off the 9/4 favourite under Paddy Brennan.

Brennan stalked the pace at the rear of the field before making smooth headway to take closer order with four furlongs to travel. The pair were soon in a prominent position and seemingly going well and took up the running well over a furlong from home. Swiftly a few lengths clear, the jockey asked the gelding to go and win his race and he stuck his head down gamely to gallop through the line strongly.

By Getaway out of a Glacial Storm mare, this is very much a staying pedigree, so it is testament to his innate ability that he has shown so much so early in his career. Hurdling will be his game this season and he should come into his own over 2m4f–3m on soft ground.

MENGLI KHAN (5YR BAY GELDING)

TRAINER:	**Gordon Elliott**
PEDIGREE:	**Lope De Vega – Danielli (Danehill)**
FORM (FLAT):	**317/4814/**
FORM (HURDLES):	**24/111O233 -**
OPTIMUM TRIP:	**2m +**
GOING:	**Soft**
HURDLES RATING:	**150**

Mengli Khan joined Gordon Elliott for the sum of 155,000gns at the back end of 2016 following a decent campaign on the Flat for Hugo Palmer.

He took time to warm to the task over obstacles but following a couple of sighters at Fairyhouse he was able to land his maiden at Navan in September 2017. He then improved further to land a Grade 3 on a revisit to the track before gaining top honours in the Grade 1 Royal Bond Novice Hurdle at Fairyhouse in December which shot him to the top of the betting for the Supreme Novices' Hurdle.

He displayed a serious quirk on his next start when to everyone's surprise he ran out at the penultimate flight in the Paddy Power Future Champions Novice Hurdle at Leopardstown and then found Getabird nine lengths too good for him in the Grade 2 Moscow Flyer Novice Hurdle at Punchestown in January.

When I saw him in the flesh at the Cheltenham Festival I was staggered by his size. He's a huge eye-filling gelding and my immediate thought was how much I'd love to see him over a fence. He fared well in the Supreme Novices' Hurdle, finishing third, beaten only two lengths on ground which was perhaps not ideal. He then rounded off his season with a third-placed effort to Draconien in the Champion Novice Hurdle at the Punchestown Festival.

THE TEN TO FOLLOW | 115

Mengli Khan – talented with the scope to progress

I am unsure of his plans for the current season, but if he is sent novice chasing he is most certainly one to keep on your side. He has already proven he can be competitive with the best two-mile novice hurdlers and, given his size, I expect him to be far more effective over fences.

Obviously, there's a lot of time between now and March but I doubt the 20/1 about him for the Arkle Chase will last long if he makes a winning chase debut.

free blogs & newsletters
www.martenjulian.com
follow the king of dark horses
@martenjulian

PALMERS HILL (5YR BAY GELDING)

TRAINER:	Jonjo O'Neill
PEDIGREE:	Gold Well – Tosca Shine (Topanoora)
FORM (P2P):	31/
FORM (HURDLE):	143 -
OPTIMUM TRIP:	2m +
GOING:	Soft
HURDLES RATING:	124

Palmers Hill is another to hail from last year's point-to-point feature following a hugely impressive 20-length victory at Tyrella after placing third in a hot maiden on his debut.

That promise from between the flags was transferred to hurdles when he won comfortably on his hurdles debut at Uttoxeter in a 2m maiden in October where he beat Enola Gay with a further gap back to Who's My Jockey in third. He then disappointed when stepped up in trip to 2m5½f at Ascot in November before being given a break only to run below par again, this time in a 2m4f novices' handicap at Sandown in February.

He ran like a non-stayer on both those occasions, but it was evident that Jonjo O'Neill's yard was under a cloud at the time and Palmers Hill may have underperformed as a result. It may just have been that the five-year-old needed time to mature and can return this season a more complete model.

Whatever the case, I remain convinced that Palmers Hill is very well handicapped on a mark of 124 and will make an impression over hurdles before switching to novice chasing.

SANTINI (6YR BAY GELDING)

TRAINER:	Nicky Henderson
PEDIGREE:	Milan – Tinagoodnight (Sleeping Car)
FORM (P2P):	1/
FORM (HURDLES):	1131 -
OPTIMUM TRIP:	2m 4f +
GOING:	Good/Soft
HURDLES RATING:	152

No prizes for imagination for including Santini in a 'horses to follow' list, but I believe this gorgeous-looking gelding could reach the very top as a novice chaser this season.

Very little was known about the 15-length winner of a Didmarton point-to-point 12 months ago, but he soon made an impact when making a winning Rules debut for Nicky Henderson at Newbury in December under Nico de Boinville. He took plenty of organising after pinging the third from home but once jumping the last he really found his stride and powered clear of his more fancied stable companion Chef Des Obeaux on the run to the line.

His next port of call was set to be Ascot but he was declared a late non-runner on account of the soft ground. He then reappeared a week later at Cheltenham in the Grade 2 Ballymore Classic Novices' Hurdle trial where, again, the ground was far from ideal and officially described as heavy. Nonetheless, Santini's class shone through and staying power appeared to win him the day as he wore down subsequent Grade 1 Mersey Novices' Hurdle winner Black Op (who made a terrible blunder at the final obstacle) on the run to the line.

Stepped up in trip to three miles for the Albert Bartlett at the Festival, he was held up well off the pace before making smooth progress on the wide outside of the field. Chivvied along at the top of the hill he still had plenty to do after jumping the second from home but responded well for stronger pressure and passed a host of rivals on the run to the last to power up the hill and finish third, never nearer than at the line.

Next time at Aintree in the Grade 1 Doom Bar Novices' Hurdle, Nico de Boinville rode him far more prominently and still appeared to have plenty of horse underneath him jumping the third from home where he took his mount across the track to the nearside rail. To Santini's great credit he stuck to his task gallantly and found extra when needed up the home straight to deny Roksana by a comfortable one and a half lengths despite losing a shoe.

Santini still appeared very backward and babyish in all his races and there should be plenty of improvement to come, not least mentally but also physically as he has a huge imposing physique.

Novice chasing looks to be the order of the day this season and given how fluently he jumped over his fences in his pointing days, teamed with the level of ability he has shown already over the obstacles, I see no reason why he won't progress into a leading 2m4f–3m novice chaser this term.

It will be tricky for Nicky Henderson to keep Santini and On The Blind Side apart, but if both reach the Festival in one piece I imagine Santini will be the JLT horse and On The Blind Side will go the RSA route.

free blogs & newsletters
www.martenjulian.com

follow the king of dark horses
@martenjulian

STORM CONTROL (5YR BAY GELDING)

TRAINER:	Kerry Lee
PEDIGREE:	September Storm – Double Dream (Double Eclipse)
FORM (P2P):	1/
FORM (HURDLE):	432 -
OPTIMUM TRIP:	3m
GOING:	Good/Soft
HURDLES RATING:	127

This is a horse to get excited about. The son of September Storm looked a dour stayer and an embryonic chaser when coming home a 20-length winner on his only start between the flags and as the cliché goes, anything he did over hurdles was a bonus.

Kerry Lee started off his career in a red-hot 2m3½f maiden hurdle at Ascot where he ran well to finish fourth behind subsequent Kempton Silver Plate winner Kildisart, King Of Realms and Oakley Hall. He then plugged on for third in a 2m2½f maiden hurdle at Exeter on unfavourable heavy ground on New Year's Day before returning to Ascot in March only to be denied by Nicky Henderson's Colonial Dreams who went on to further success and is now rated 131.

Storm Control is currently rated on a mark of 127 and with a step up to three miles likely to see improvement, connections may be tempted to aim him at a handicap hurdle before embarking on a novice chase campaign. He was entered for a Grade 1 over hurdles in early January which indicates the high esteem in which he is held.

He's a very genuine individual with a very slick action over his obstacles, just as he showed over fences in his point-to-point.

Three-mile staying chases will be his bag and I can't imagine he'll remain a maiden under Rules for much longer.

TIME TO MOVE ON (5YR CHESTNUT GELDING)

TRAINER:	Fergal O'Brien
PEDIGREE:	Flemensfirth – Kapricia Speed (Vertical Speed)
FORM (BUMPER):	11 -
OPTIMUM TRIP:	2m 4f +
GOING:	Soft

Time To Move On is very much a staying chaser for further down the line, but already twice a winner of bumpers he can develop into a decent hurdler over a trip before switching codes.

The attractive, rangy son of Flemensfirth made an instant impact on his debut in a well-contested bumper at Exeter in December under Barry Geraghty. He travelled into the race moving powerfully two furlongs from home and eased effortlessly to the front before putting the race to bed in a matter of strides once asked for an effort inside the final furlong. Market leader Caribert, who came into the race full of confidence after winning on his debut, had no response for Time To Move On and trailed home 10 lengths behind but has subsequently gone on to win the Goffs UK Spring Sales Bumper. A further enhancement of the form came from Henry Daly's fifth-placed Stoney Mountain and ninth-placed Snuff Box.

The five-year-old wasn't as visually impressive on his return to Exeter, where he defied his penalty on heavy ground, but he always looked in control despite idling and taking a good look around on the run to the line.

By Flemensfirth out of a Vertical Speed mare, he is a half-brother to stable stalwart Barney Dwan who runs for the same connections. He is also a full brother to Michael Scudamore's bumper/2m6f/2m7f hurdle winner Cadeyrn.

Time To Move On possesses plenty of size and looks likely to develop into a smart chaser in future. He is also a bit of a character in his stable and likes things on his terms.

He ought to relish trips in excess of 2m4f and could develop into one of the stable's leading novices this term.

WILHELM VONVENSTER (4YR BAY GELDING)

TRAINER:	Nicky Richards
PEDIGREE:	Apsis – Princesse Gaelle (Osorio)
FORM:	Unraced
OPTIMUM TRIP:	2m +
GOING:	Good to Soft

This is by far the darkest name on the list but I believe he is a horse we'll be hearing plenty more about over the coming season.

Wilhelm Vonvenster first came to my attention over 12 months ago when I saw him at Nicky Richards' yard a couple of weeks

Nicky Richards – master of Greystoke

after he and Gerry Griffin bought him for €28,000 at the Goffs Land Rover National Hunt Sale. There were a few horses that day to poke their heads over their box doors, but this son of Apsis had a great presence and instantly took my eye.

He is a good-looking, well-made gelding with a decent amount of power to his frame. Bred on French flat lines, his dam Princesse Gaelle placed twice up to 1m3f for Marco Botti before winning on the Flat in France and later over hurdles. The further family link back to Grade 2 French Flat 10.5f Listed and 1m7f Group 2 winner Celtic Celebre.

Nicky likes to bring his horses along slowly, but when I saw the gelding at the yard in September he looked plenty forward enough and will most likely be making his debut in a bumper in the early part of the season.

Marten's Latest News

If you want to keep in touch with Marten's latest thoughts ring him on:

0906 150 1555

Selections given in the first minute

Calls charged at £1.50 a minute at all times & your telecom provider will add their own Access Charge. Please contact your provider for their charges.

Telephone & Text Service

A non-premium rate version of this line is available. Please call the office if you'd like to join or order online. The line is an 03 number which is the same as calling a landline and included in a mobile phone package. Marten sends a text message direct each day. Prices also available online.

THE 2019 CHAMPION HURDLE PREVIEW

MARTEN JULIAN

Buveur D'Air is currently a top price of 7/2 to win the Champion Hurdle for a third successive year.

Nicky Henderson's seven-year-old will be trying to follow in the footsteps of some great names of the past – Persian War, See You Then and Istabraq – to land a hat-trick of victories in jump racing's top hurdling crown.

Yet even at this early stage of the season – writing in September – the son of Crillon appears likely to face his stiffest task to date.

Buveur D'Air only just prevailed in last year's race. Having taken the lead approaching the second last, he was upsides Melon approaching the final flight and was headed for a few strides on the run-in until bravely battling back to lead towards the finish, winning by a neck.

The narrowness of his margin of victory can probably be attributed to the heavy ground. This was only the second time he had encountered such going, officially described, the other occasion being when he beat the gallant but inferior Rayvin Black at Sandown in February 2017.

Barry Geraghty described the ground afterwards as "very tacky down the back straight", adding, that he tried to "save as much as I could to go as late as possible". Nicky Henderson has since added that he feels the horse was "not at his very best".

This was the first time for a while that Buveur D'Air had to dig deep.

In what was a rough race from the home turn – he leant on both Faugheen and Melon approaching the second last – it was

Buveur D'Air – a gentle stroll

the horse's stamina that came to his aid. Like many of the top Champion Hurdle winners of recent years, Buveur D'Air has shown Grade 1 winning form over two and a half miles.

Nicky Henderson, who has handled the horse with such skill over the years, says the horse requires plenty of work to get fit. That is why he was keen to run him at Sandown in February having already landed the Fighting Fifth in December and the Christmas Hurdle at Kempton – races that will again be on his agenda.

The trainer says the Champion Hurdle will be his ultimate target and, to quote the old adage, he is the one they have to beat.

The overriding question, as I write in the autumn, relates to the plans for **Samcro**.

The son of Germany is currently unbeaten in seven completed starts, having travelled through his races with great ease and invariably finding a turn of foot in the closing stages.

The problem is that on the one occasion he was tried outside novice company – at Punchestown in April in a race that was intended to guide connections to the way forward – he tipped up when going well three from home.

It is open to debate what the outcome would have been, but given the way he powered home in the Ballymore Novices' Hurdle over an extended 2m 5f and, indeed, the authority with which he had always finished his races, he probably had plenty still to give.

Samcro – triumphant

Samcro, in common with all the Gigginstown horses, was bought to be a chaser. Now a six-year-old, he is the right age to make the transition to fences. The owners would probably like him to move on to the next stage but I suspect Gordon Elliott thinks otherwise.

The trainer would love to win a Champion Hurdle and Samcro would be his best chance since he took out a licence. Apparently no decision has yet been made, but assuming that he would have stayed hurdling had he won at Punchestown I expect the plan will be to start him over hurdles and see how it goes.

They will probably also keep a watch on how the other contenders are getting on in their early-season forays.

If I owned Samcro I would keep him to hurdles for his first couple of starts, hopefully finding a race where he faced a decent horse or two. If he looked vulnerable then he could switch to chasing before Christmas.

Samcro is generally a good jumper who stays beyond two miles and handles testing ground. For all the praise heaped upon him he still has to prove himself outside novice company.

One of the most intriguing aspects of the 2018 Cheltenham Festival was the strength of market support in the Champion Hurdle for **Melon**.

This was a proper old-fashioned gamble and it almost came off. Backed from 14/1, bigger in places, to 7/1, the six-year-old looked like prevailing halfway up the run-in until the winner fought back bravely to head into the lead close home.

Melon has always shown top-class form without suggesting he was a champion. Runner-up to the enigmatic Labaik in the 2017 Supreme Novices' Hurdle, he ran third to My Tent Or Yours at Cheltenham in December before running fifth of eight, beaten 12 lengths by Supasundae, at Leopardstown in February when hooded for the first time.

Melon – gave favourite backers a big fright

That form suggested the horse had no more than an outside chance of winning the Champion Hurdle, but the market support proved spot on and he was in the process of running another good race at Punchestown in April only to fall upsides Samcro three hurdles from home.

Willie Mullins says that Melon has always worked well at home and he will be kept hurdling this season with, one assumes, the Champion Hurdle as his back-end target.

On the book, with doubts about the participation of Samcro, a case can be made for suggesting he represents fair each-way value at 8/1.

The award for the gamest performance seen at last year's Festival has to go to **Summerville Boy**, who won the opening Supreme Novices' Hurdle.

The race is always a serious test of a novice, run at a furious pace with no quarter given, but even by past standards the 2018 renewal was a particularly challenging contest.

Noel Fehily had Summerville Boy tucked away at the back for the first mile of the race before weaving his way through the pack down the far side. He moved up threateningly to within three lengths of the leaders before what looked a calamitous blunder at the second last, costing him five lengths, at least that many places and all momentum.

The horse's chance looked lost and once in the straight he was still out of his ground, approaching the final hurdle about six lengths adrift of the leader. He then clattered the last, again losing ground and momentum, before remarkably putting his head down to challenge the gutsy Kalashnikov and get up close home and win by a neck.

I cannot recall ever before seeing a novice hurdler prevail over such adversity at this meeting. It was a performance of extraordinary tenacity, especially for a novice in such heavy ground. The performance confirmed the winner's superiority over the runner-up, having beaten him by four lengths at Sandown. These efforts were a marked step up on his first three runs, when he had been beaten.

THE 2019 CHAMPION HURDLE PREVIEW

Summerville Boy – exceptionally tough

This scopey six-year-old can be keen so a strongly run race suits him well. His family is made up of point-to-point winners and staying hurdlers and chasers so, given his style of racing, he should have no problem with stepping up in trip provided he has a strong pace.

As for the Champion Hurdle, I am not sure his courage is sufficient to pose a threat to Buveur D'Air.

The testing ground in March probably brought his stamina into play while he needs to polish up his jumping to be competitive in a Champion Hurdle field.

For all that, this is a horse of admirable courage and that, alone, will ensure he proves competitive at any level.

To the eye, few horses were as visually impressive at last year's Festival as **Laurina**.

The daughter of Spanish Moon had shaped well in two starts in France in April 2017. She then made her debut for Willie Mullins at Tramore in December, winning by 15 lengths, before landing a Grade 3 by 11 lengths at Fairyhouse in January.

Laurina – a great talent with more to offer

Those runs set her up for the Trull House Stud Mares' Novices' Hurdle at Cheltenham, where she was heavily backed to 4/7 and beat Cap Soleil by 18 lengths. Her season ended with another facile win in a Grade 1 over 2m4f at Fairyhouse in April.

Laurina is a sizeable mare who, according to Paul Townend, rides more like a gelding. She stays well and loves testing ground. The concern in relation to this race is two miles on a quicker surface. She is also prone to the occasional sloppy jump.

There is the possibility that she could be aimed at the mares' programme, something her trainer has done in the past.

Laurina is undeniably useful but we need to see how she copes outside novice company before thinking of her in terms of the Champion Hurdle.

Stable companion **Min** looks set to continue his chasing career at a high level following a successful season in novice company. It would be a surprise to see him revert to hurdling.

Supasundae has matured into a versatile hurdler, equally adept at two miles to three. The ground turned against him for the Stayers' Hurdle, where he ran second to Penhill, and he then found L'Ami Serge too smart for him over 2m4f at Aintree before taking advantage of the falls of Samcro and Melon in the Champion Hurdle at Punchestown.

Supasundae improved last season and as his recent record shows he is a very hard horse to keep out of the frame. A Champion Hurdle challenge seems unlikely but if others fall by the wayside he could be allowed to take his chance.

It has to be highly doubtful that we will see **Faugheen** in the line-up. He will be 11 in March and was comfortably outpointed by Buveur D'Air, beaten 22 lengths, before showing his appreciation of the step up to three miles when beating Penhill by 13 lengths at Punchestown in April.

Faugheen's record, which reads 14 wins and two seconds from 18 starts, stands up to the closest inspection but he's a delicate

Supasundae – versatile and reliable

sort and it's hard to see him having the constitution to cope with the pressures of a Champion Hurdle.

We Have A Dream ran off a sequence of five victories last season, leaving connections pondering a tilt at this year's Champion Hurdle.

The four-year-old son of Martaline made all to win three of his first four starts but had to miss the Triumph Hurdle at

Cheltenham due to sickness. He came back for the Grade 1 Doom Bar Anniversary Hurdle at Aintree in April and stayed on well to beat Gumball by seven lengths.

The four-year-old's rating of 156 reflects the gulf between him and the leading contenders but the Champion Hurdle is the logical next step and he still looks on an upward curve.

Stable companion **My Tent Or Yours** will be 12 in March but latest reports suggest he stays in training. Runner-up in three Champion Hurdles, he missed last season's race having returned with a gallant defeat of The New One in the Unibet International Hurdle in December.

That race will again be his first target.

We Have A Dream – won five last season

Mick Jazz made progress last season, starting in November from a mark of 144 and ending the campaign on 162 having run the best race of his career to finish third in the Champion Hurdle, beaten just three and a quarter lengths.

Before that fine effort he ran third to Supasundae in the Irish Champion Hurdle having won the Grade 1 Ryanair Hurdle at Leopardstown over Christmas.

It would be unwise to underestimate Mick Jazz's Champion Hurdle run. He may have started 25/1 but he was travelling better than Buveur D'Air and Melon turning for home having put in a particularly fluent round of jumping.

Mick Jazz – a very live outsider

It has to be conceded that Mick Jazz travels well through a race but doesn't always find much off the bridle – something his trainer Gordon Elliott acknowledges – but he is ideally suited to a strong pace, as he found in the Champion Hurdle, and he may be the type of horse that can run well in the race again.

Assuming he stays hurdling I could make out a case for him at 33/1 to make the frame again.

Saldier showed a bright turn of foot to beat Mr Adjudicator by three lengths in the Champion Four Year Old Hurdle at Punchestown in April. He had finished 23 lengths behind the runner-up when they met in the Triumph Hurdle and this performance saw his mark rise from 133 to 152.

It will be interesting to see how Saldier is campaigned given the degree of improvement he showed in that final run.

Mengli Khan is an imposing beast with the scope to progress, but he has never been straightforward – as we saw when he ran out two flights from home at Leopardstown over Christmas – but his form when beaten two lengths by Summerville Boy at Cheltenham puts him in with a squeak.

A useful sort on the Flat, it is not beyond the realms of possibility that he could ease his way into the Champion Hurdle picture.

CONCLUSION

It is not easy trying to assess this race without knowing about the participation of Samcro. Although he has yet to prove himself outside novice class, he has the potential to be something special. However at a best price of 4/1, as I write in the autumn, he does not tempt.

Buveur D'Air is a 'safe pair of hands' in that his preparatory races are virtually set in stone and he's been there and done it twice, showing last spring that he has the courage to match his talent. At 7/2 he is probably worth a saving bet.

Melon is interesting at 8/1. I am not sure that he can win a Champion Hurdle, especially as he might have come up against a slightly out of sorts favourite in last year's race, but at the price he is reasonable each-way value.

The one that could also be of interest is Mick Jazz. His current price of 33/1 is disrespectful given his fine effort last season. Yes he needs to improve again, but Gordon Elliott has worked wonders in the past couple of years and the seven-year-old could make up the leeway with the favourite, especially on better ground.

I suggest Mick Jazz and Melon, at 33/1 and 8/1 respectively. Buveur D'Air is the saving bet at 7/2.

Marten Julian

Marten's Latest News

If you want to keep in touch with Marten's latest thoughts ring him on:

0906 150 1555

Selections given in the first minute

Calls charged at £1.50 a minute at all times & your telecom provider will add their own Access Charge. Please contact your provider for their charges.

Telephone & Text Service

A non-premium rate version of this line is available. Please call the office if you'd like to join or order online. The line is an 03 number which is the same as calling a landline and included in a mobile phone package. Marten sends a text message direct each day. Prices also available online.

THE 2019 CHELTENHAM GOLD CUP PREVIEW

MARTEN JULIAN

I am probably not alone in taking the view that the untypically soft ground had a major bearing on the result of the 2018 Cheltenham Gold Cup.

Many will argue that the 94th running of this great race was not a vintage renewal – less than a stone on official ratings separated the top-rated from the lowest – but as a spectacle it was a purist's delight, with the two market leaders galloping upsides toe for toe for much of the extended 3m 2f trip.

I suggested in last year's *Guide* that if the ground were to ride soft on Gold Cup day then Native River, who finished third to Sizing John and Minella Rocco in 2017, would come into his own. By contrast I argued that Might Bite's stamina could be compromised by the combination of the trip, track and testing ground. That is probably how things came to pass.

From flagfall **Native River** and Might Bite had the race to themselves. At no stage did any of the other 13 opponents get a look in.

Richard Johnson, whose assertive style of riding is ideally suited to Native River, decided to set the pace in the knowledge that his mount would relish the test. The eight-year-old jumped in his usual manner – safe, without being spectacular, and a little to his right. Tracked throughout by Nico de Boinville on Might Bite, for much of the way it looked as if the leader was giving the 4/1 favourite the perfect lead.

Turning down the hill for home, Native River came under pressure while Might Bite still seemed to be on the bridle, poised to pounce and ease ahead. For a few strides approaching the second last that seemed likely until, approaching the final fence, Johnson encouraged his mount to dig for more and to the horse's great credit he began to pull clear again, comfortably holding the runner-up by four and a half lengths at the line.

That was the furthest Native River was clear of Might Bite at any stage of the race, with the respective stamina of both horses – in the conditions – apparently playing a major role in the outcome.

It was only the second time since Desert Orchid's memorable defeat of Yahoo back in 1989 that the race time, in this case 7 mins 2.60 secs, was over seven minutes. The other occasion was the 7 mins 5.06 secs recorded by Bobs Worth in 2013.

Cheltenham – an air of expectancy

Native River is an admirable racehorse in every way.

An old-fashioned type, trained by Colin Tizzard and his son in the traditional way, he was a decent 145-rated hurdler when he switched to fences, but chasing was always going to be his game. In that sphere he has run 13 times, never out of the first three, winning eight, second once and third four times.

He left no doubt that stamina was his forte when, as a six-year-old at the 2016 Festival, he ran Minella Rocco to one and a quarter lengths in the 4m National Hunt Chase, closing on the winner all the way to the line.

The following season he won the Hennessy from a mark of 155 before staying on dourly to win the Coral Welsh National from the same mark. In the Gold Cup nearly three months later he again did strong late work to finish third to Sizing John, not able to dominate from the front as he did in March.

A setback kept him off the course for the early part of last season until his return in the Betfair Denman Chase at Newbury, where he gave 3lb to the reliable Cloudy Dream and beat him 12 lengths.

The horse enjoyed a trouble-free preparation – "perfect", in the words of his trainer – in the weeks leading to Cheltenham after which it was decided to put him away for the summer.

Things may be busier for him this time around, with connections apparently keen to try and land the £1 million bonus for the horse that wins the Betfair Chase at Haydock on 24 November, the King George at Kempton on Boxing Day and the Gold Cup.

Native River is a sound jumper, who has never fallen, and is very consistent. He is also still progressive, now rated on 176 – 10lb higher than at the start of last season.

It is, though, important for him to have ease in the ground when competing at the highest level. That is not to say he cannot win another Gold Cup on good ground, but the greater

Native River – an admirable racehorse in every way

the emphasis on stamina the better it will suit him.

Native River is a thoroughly likeable performer who has been well served by both his jockey and his trainer. Given his favoured conditions it is inconceivable that he will not, again, have a major part to play.

Apparently Nice de Boinville was castigating himself after his defeat on **Might Bite**, wondering if he could have done things any differently.

It's easy to understand his frustration, having been given a handy lead through the race and sitting there with what seemed a double handful turning for home.

Might Bite had made all to beat Whisper by a couple of lengths over 3m 1f at Aintree in April 2017, but this extra furlong and a half up the demanding Cheltenham hill on soft ground presents a far stiffer test and the son of Scorpion found less than had looked likely three fences from home.

Just under a month later the nine-year-old went back to Aintree to win the Grade 1 Betway Bowl Chase by seven lengths from Bristol De Mai, a race just shy of 3m 1f run on good to soft ground.

Before Cheltenham Might Bite landed the King George VI Chase at Kempton, the race his trainer Nicky Henderson had long nominated as his main target of the season up to that point. His defeat there of 151-rated Double Shuffle and Tea For Two left many questioning the value of the form, but with Thistlecrack, Whisper and Bristol De Mai stretched out behind – and on ground softer than ideal – that criticism seems harsh.

It is well documented that Might Bite has not always been straightforward.

Might Bite – 25/1 to land the £1 million bonus

He almost threw away his winning advantage in the 2017 RSA Novices' Chase when veering sharply right on the run-in, and some raised concerns that the return to Prestbury Park might precipitate the same reaction.

Such fears proved unfounded, and in fact since that day in 2017 his behaviour has been impeccable, with four emphatic successes and just the one defeat in the Gold Cup, where again he kept perfectly straight.

Might Bite has been made 25/1 to land the Jockey Club £1 million bonus, favourite ahead of 33/1 chance Native River. Kauto Star proved it could be done in 2010, while Cue Card landed the first two legs before falling in his Gold Cup.

It is my view that their respective market positions are correct because the ground is, historically, more likely to be good for most of those races than testing.

As for the Gold Cup, I expect Might Bite to reverse the form with the winner on good ground or quicker. The top price of 13/2 is reasonable as with a clear run and typical spring ground – and factoring in the strong following the horse enjoys – I would expect him to start favourite.

The chief market threat to the two principals is **Presenting Percy**, a seven-year-old trained by Pat Kelly in Ireland.

Rated 157 as a hurdler, having won the 2017 Pertemps Network Final from a mark of 146, he has since run five times over fences, winning three and placed on the other two occasions.

The highlight of his season was a defeat of Monalee in the RSA Chase where, under a typical stalking ride from the hugely talented Davy Russell, he came from arrears to win going away. That followed a gutsy second to Our Duke over 2m 4f in the Red Mills Chase at Gowran Park.

Official BHA figures have Presenting Percy on a mark of 165 – 7lb below Might Bite and 11lb behind Native River. He is, though, the youngest of the three and the least experienced.

Presenting Percy – waiting in the wings

His trainer Pat Kelly is highly respected by his peers and the horse has stamina in plentiful supply, having won a handicap chase over 3m 5f at Fairyhouse in December 2017.

I do, though, have one serious concern with this horse and that is his jumping.

Although he has never fallen he tends to jump rather flat. He gets a little close to the top of the fences although, in his defence, it does not appear to cost him momentum.

He may improve as he gains experience, but at championship pace over a distance of ground he will need to.

What should work in his favour is his stealthy style of racing.

Both Might Bite and Native River like to be up with the pace and that could set the scene for a closer. In that respect

Presenting Percy fills the bill, while his proven stamina and versatility regarding ground – he has won on good and heavy – are also strongly to his advantage.

When **Footpad** was born to this world his breeders almost certainly had something other than the Gold Cup in mind.

A son of 2008 Lockinge Stakes winner Creachadoir out of a mare by Sadler's Wells, his unbeaten run of five victories over fences now sees him standing as fourth favourite at 16/1 for the Gold Cup.

Footpad – a great leaper but how far will he stay?

Trainer Willie Mullins hinted that the horse could be a little bit special after his debut chasing win at Navan in November, telling the scribes assembled afterwards that the horse's schooling at home had been "as good as any novice we've had".

That view was vindicated when, in the main, he jumped well in his five chases. He did make one notable mistake at the sixth in the Arkle Challenge Trophy but still went on to beat the talented but mercurial Brain Power by 14 lengths, powering away after the last.

Regarding his stamina for the Gold Cup, Footpad was placed third but well beaten when he tackled three miles over hurdles in April 2017 and he does not appeal as a natural stayer.

He is bred for the Flat and has a nimble and pacy way of racing. His mark of 166 puts him within reach of the best, but the Queen Mother Champion Chase or Ryanair would appeal as more obvious targets unless the Mullins team is short of other options for the Gold Cup, which seems unlikely.

Sizing John belied my personal concerns that the trip would prove beyond him when beating Minella Rocco and Native River in the 2017 Gold Cup, finding the good ground to his liking. He returned last season with a seven-length defeat of Djakadam in the 2m 4f Grade 1 John Durkan Memorial Chase at Punchestown but was then found to be clinically abnormal after being beaten 32 lengths in the Christmas Chase at Leopardstown.

Trainer Jessica Harrington thought she had the horse back to full fitness in time for the Festival until announcing a week before the race that the horse was suffering with a pelvic injury. The plan was to give him a fortnight's box rest and then time off for the summer.

Sizing John became the third consecutive Gold Cup winner following Coneygree and Don Cossack to miss the following year's race.

Sizing John – being nursed back to full health

Aged just eight, Sizing John will be given every opportunity to make a full recovery. He is currently rated on 169 and was two and three-quarter lengths ahead of Native River in the 2017 Gold Cup, so we know that on collateral lines of form he is up there with the market leaders. Latest reports suggest his trainer is very keen to get him back there in March.

The Gold Cup seems the natural target for **Bellshill**.

The eight-year-old son of King's Theatre has been to three of the last four Festivals, starting with an appearance in the 2015 Champion Bumper. He finished in mid-division there and a year later he came home last but one to Altior in the Supreme Novices' Hurdle.

Switched to fences at the start of the following season he ran a decent third to Might Bite in the RSA Novices' Chase. Things started off well for him belatedly last season, with an odds-on victory over 3m 1f at Fairyhouse in February and then he showed that stamina was his strong suit in finishing fifth of 30 (disqualified from fourth), beaten just a length, over the demanding 3m 5f of the Irish Grand National in heavy ground.

His season ended with a three-quarter-length defeat of Djakadam in the Punchestown Gold Cup over an extended three miles in April.

Bellshill is all about stamina, despite having won races over short of three miles. A mark of 168 leaves him a few pounds adrift of the top, a view confirmed on lines through Djakadam. Owners Andrea and Graham Wylie will be keen to see their colours represented on the big day and the Gold Cup would be the logical target for the horse, but it would probably need to be soft to see him take a hand.

Shattered Love is an interesting prospect.

Gordon Elliott's daughter of Yeats has a touch of speed in her bottom line – her dam is an unraced half-sister to Champion Hurdle winner Make A Stand – but she showed she could stay three miles when beating Jury Duty on her fifth start over fences in a Grade 1 novice chase at Leopardstown in December 2017.

She was then kept fresh for the Festival and rewarded the patience shown by connections when beating Terrefort by seven lengths in the JLT Novices' Chase over the greater part of two and a half miles.

Just over a fortnight later she found Al Boum Photo a length too good for her over 2m 4f at Fairyhouse before finishing fifth of 11 to The Storyteller over an extended three miles at Punchestown.

Shattered Love – no forlorn hope at 25/1

Shattered Love, who is rated on 153, is a very gutsy mare with the stamina to win over an extended three miles and the pace to win at shorter distances. She is versatile regarding ground and will be aged just eight in March. She will also qualify for the mares' allowance.

Shattered Love has only once finished out of the first two in eight starts over fences – her lifetime record reads just three of her 17 starts out of the three. The mare needs to improve but could not be in better hands to do so. At 25/1 she is not unattractively priced so monitor her progress closely, especially with regard to forthcoming plans.

Road To Respect has over 12 lengths to find with Native River on their Gold Cup form last season. He was then comfortably outpointed, after a sequence of careless jumps, by Bellshill in the Grade 1 Punchestown Gold Cup.

There is no valid reason why he should not find the stone required to measure up with the market leaders – he won the 2m 5f handicap at the meeting from a mark of 145 in 2017 – but he's an awkward jumper and makes limited appeal.

Thistlecrack, who will be aged 11 next March, has apparently made a full recovery from the setback which kept him off the track for the second half of last season.

The son of Kayf Tara looked imperious when winning the 2016 Stayers' Hurdle by seven lengths before following up at Aintree in April. His novice chase season started well enough with victories at Chepstow, Cheltenham and Newbury before

Thistlecrack – greeting the dawn

beating Cue Card in the 2016 King George VI Chase. That was followed by a memorable tussle with the ill-fated Many Clouds in the Cotswold Chase at Cheltenham in January over an extended 3m 1f, a battle he lost by a head.

Last season started with a quiet run over hurdles at Newbury before a respectable fourth to Might Bite at Kempton on Boxing Day. He then sustained a stress fracture which kept him off the track for the remainder of the season.

The four-time Grade 1-winning hurdler has the Charlie Hall Chase at Wetherby on 3 November as his first target, with a view to then tackling the £1 million bonus. Connections say the horse is now over his problems.

That may be the case, but for all his latent talent he may find younger legs have the better of him.

Douvan is another that has to prove he has recovered from a troubled season.

A top-class hurdler, who won the Supreme Novices' Hurdle in 2015, he then switched to chasing and was unbeaten in his first nine starts over fences, six of them at Grade 1 level including a seven-length defeat of Sizing John in the 2016 Arkle Trophy.

The following season he won his first three races, again beating Sizing John, before flopping at odds of 2/9 in the Queen Mother Champion Chase. He was subsequently found to have sustained an injury to his pelvis.

That was the last we were to see of him until the Festival last March, when he returned for another crack at the Queen Mother Champion Chase. For much of the race he looked like the Douvan of old, jumping well and travelling strongly, until he fell four fences from home.

Next time out he came up against stable companion Un De Sceaux in the 2m Champion Chase at Punchestown. Rated 8lb superior, and heavily supported to 4/5, he seemed to be travelling as well as ever for much of the race until his jumping

Douvan – will he return?

became more wayward over the last five fences. Despite staying on well he was never going to catch Un De Sceaux and went down by three and three-quarter lengths.

There are two very obvious concerns about Douvan.

The first is obviously his wellbeing. He did not look at ease with himself in the closing stages at Punchestown while his fall at Cheltenham can't have helped matters.

The second is his stamina. The son of Walk In The Park has never raced beyond 2m 1f, and although he was winning his races with plenty in hand he has always had loads of pace.

In my view Douvan will return, but he would have to prove he is fighting fit and back to something close to his best to warrant a crack at the Gold Cup.

Most years a horse from 'left field' emerges as a contender and this season that role could be filled by **Waiting Patiently**, who is trained by Ruth Jefferson following the untimely death in February of her father Malcolm.

The winner of one of his three starts over hurdles, he switched to chasing in the autumn of 2016 and quickly showed that was his game, winning novice chases off 123, 136 and 142.

Waiting Patiently – a live outsider

He then missed the remainder of the campaign and returned in a 2m 4f Listed chase at Carlisle in November, beating Belami Des Pictons by two and a half lengths. Just over two months later he went to Kempton to win a Listed chase over an extended 2m 4f before a memorable defeat of Cue Card in the Grade 1 Betfair Ascot Chase.

Soft ground is imperative for this son of Flemensfirth. Given such conditions he can travel and quicken. As for his stamina, his full brother Walking In The Air won a point-to-point and over 2m 5f over hurdles and their dam is a half-sister to winners over three miles and more.

It's a close call, but taking into account how well the horse travels and settles, I believe he will stay three miles and quite possibly the longer trip at Cheltenham. As for his form, a rating of 170 leaves him just 6lb adrift of Native River and 2lb behind Might Bite.

The horse is reported to be back in fine fettle and on ratings he should not be a 33/1 chance. The ground is a concern, but on form he should not be at such long odds and I put his name forward as one of the best value outsiders in the race.

Al Boum Photo did well to concede the 7lb mares' allowance to Shattered Love in the Grade 1 2m 4f Ryanair Gold Cup Novice Chase at Fairyhouse in April before an extraordinary incident in the extended 3m Champion Novice Chase at Punchestown, when Paul Townend inexplicably steered him across the track, when leading, in an apparent attempt to bypass the final fence.

That race seemed to confirm that the horse stays three miles and his form with The Storyteller and Shattered Love reads well. He may do enough to earn the right to make the line-up.

Terrefort is another that could creep into contention. A consistent performer in France, he ran four times for Nicky

Henderson last season winning three and progressing from a mark of 137 to 158.

There was no disgrace in his sole defeat, when second to Shattered Love at Cheltenham, before ending the season with a three and three-quarter length defeat of the talented Ms Parfois on his first attempt over 3m 1f at Aintree in April.

The horse is expected to thrive under the tutelage of his masterful handler.

Killultagh Vic failed to complete in three of his five starts last season, tailed off and then pulled up in the Gold Cup. The winner of the Martin Pipe Conditional Jockeys' Handicap Hurdle at the 2015 Festival from a mark of 135, he has run just five times over fences and appears to be both temperamentally and physically unsound.

Monalee has the scope to progress. The son of Milan was a useful novice staying hurdler, notably running second to Penhill in the 2017 Albert Bartlett Novices' Hurdle, but it was evident that chasing would be his game when he jumped well to make a winning debut over fences at Punchestown in November.

He was then a close third when falling at the 10th fence in the race won by Shattered Love at Leopardstown before making all to beat Al Boum Photo over 2m 5f back there in February. He was beaten on merit by Presenting Percy at Cheltenham before tipping over three fences from home in The Storyteller's race at Punchestown in April.

Monalee is young enough to progress but he has something to find with Presenting Percy and others.

Bristol De Mai seems to have been around a long time for his seven years.

The talented grey looks a world-beater on his day, and that particular day is when the ground is hock-deep at Haydock. His 57-length defeat of Cue Card in the Betfair Chase last November ranks as one of the single most impressive performances seen by a chaser anywhere last season, but he could not replicate that form a month later in the King George and then ran third to Definitly Red at Cheltenham. He then had wind surgery but returned with a sound runner-up spot to Might Bite at Aintree.

Bristol De Mai is as good as anything when he has conditions to suit, but he was well beaten by Sizing John in the 2017 Gold Cup and he is most unlikely to get his underfoot conditions at Cheltenham in March. He is, though, still a relatively young horse and there are more big pots to be won with him.

Disko – a serious player if he gets back to full fitness

We didn't see anything of **Disko** after his return to action at Down Royal in November. The seven-year-old has only once finished out of the frame in 12 lifetime starts having enjoyed a fine campaign in 2016/17, notably running a good third to Yorkhill in the JLT Novices' Chase at Cheltenham.

Defeats of Our Duke at Leopardstown and last spring's Gold Cup third Anibale Fly, over an extended three miles at Punchestown, show him in a very favourable light.

You never know whether they will return to top form after injury but Disko – who endured another accident during the summer – certainly has the ability to become a contender and, aged just seven, he is entitled to progress.

Clan Des Obeaux has the potential to work his way up the ranks.

The six-year-old son of Kapgarde ran Whisper to half-a-length as a novice chaser at Cheltenham in January 2017, and all was going well last season with a victory at Haydock in November and a couple of good runs at Kempton and Cheltenham until he threw a splint.

He missed the Festival but got back in time for Aintree, when he ran third beaten just over 10 lengths by Might Bite in the Betway Bowl Chase despite a rushed preparation.

He is young enough to make up the leeway on the winner and is one to keep an eye on. The plan is to start him in the Charlie Hall Chase at Wetherby.

Last year's Gold Cup third **Anibale Fly** was doing all his best work in the closing stages of the race. It was a similar story next time in the Grand National where, over a mile further, he plugged on steadily at the finish. The eight-year-old is a sound jumper but a dyed-in-the-wool stayer and things may again happen a little too quickly for him next March.

Fox Norton disappeared from the scene after pulling up in the King George VI Chase at Kempton. That was his first attempt at three miles, having run Politologue to half a length in the Tingle Creek Chase at Sandown and made an impressive return when beating Cloudy Dream by five lengths at Cheltenham in November.

The plan had been to tackle the Ryanair Chase at Cheltenham but a suspensory injury kept him off the track for the rest of the season.

Minella Rocco, who ran second to Sizing John in 2017, was being aimed at the Grand National last season only for him to be withdrawn on account of the soft ground. The eight-year-old has had a hobday and soft palate operation and Aintree, rather than Cheltenham, will again be the main target.

Ms Parfois, rated 146, is over two stone adrift of the top contenders but she has tenacity and commitment in abundance and it is not beyond the realms of possibility that a good run of form before Christmas may earn her a Gold Cup entry. She stays extremely well.

Coney Island had close form with Our Duke and Anibale Fly in 2016 and came from way behind to beat Adrien Du Pont on his return at Ascot in December. He was pulled up on his next two starts but he is young enough to improve and is likely to come back this season a fresh horse.

CONCLUSION

Native River is hard to fault but there can be no doubt he is at his most effective on easy ground and he will require those conditions to win the Gold Cup for a second time.

Might Bite, who now seems to have his temperamental issues behind him, is expected to reverse the form on better ground. Given a good run through the season and appropriate ground conditions on the day I expect him to start favourite.

My concern with Presenting Percy is his jumping although from a tactical perspective the strong pace of the race will play to his strengths. I don't expect Footpad to prove fully effective over the trip while Sizing John and Thistlecrack have to prove they are back to full health.

Douvan is an exceptional talent but there are health and stamina worries about him.

For value, at 25/1 and 33/1 respectively, take a look at the consistent Shattered Love and Waiting Patiently. The latter would prefer soft ground but on figures he should not be at such long odds. Disko and Clan Des Obeaux are others that could enter the reckoning.

Might Bite has the class to win a Gold Cup provided the ground is to his liking. Native River's exceptional resolution will ensure he always has a part to play and of the others, with trading value in mind, I suggest Shattered Love and Waiting Patiently.

Marten's Latest News

If you want to keep in touch with Marten's latest thoughts ring him on:

0906 150 1555

Selections given in the first minute

Calls charged at £1.50 a minute at all times & your telecom provider will add their own Access Charge. Please contact your provider for their charges.

Telephone & Text Service

A non-premium rate version of this line is available. Please call the office if you'd like to join or order online. The line is an 03 number which is the same as calling a landline and included in a mobile phone package. Marten sends a text message direct each day. Prices also available online.

INDEX

Acey Milan 9-11
Adjali 25
Air De Rock 55
Al Boum Photo 153
Andy Dufresne 69-70
Anibale Fly 156
Annamix 25-26
Arrowtown 26
Aye Aye Charlie 11-12
Ballymoy 103-104
Battleoverdoyen 106
Behind Time 56-57
Bellshill 146-147
Beyondthestorm 27-28
Black Op 107-109
Blackbow 100
Brewin'Upastorm 102, 109-110
Bristol De Mai 154-155
Bulls Head 28
Buveur D'Air 123-125
Cadeyrn 29-30
Carefully Selected 101
Caribert 13
Champ 30
Champagne Platinum 70-72
Chante Neige 31
Checkitout 72-73
Chooseyourweapon 104
Clan Des Obeaux 156
Clarendon Street 32
Coney Island 157
Cool Getaway 106
Copper Gone West 106
Court Liability 103
Cracking Destiny 100
Deja Vue 74

Disko 155-156
Dlauro 76-77
Dolos 14-15
Dorrells Pierji 101
Douvan 150-151
Downtown Getaway 32-33
Duhallow Gesture 111-112
Eden Du Houx 78-79
El Barra 33
El Kaldoun 34
Elysees 34-35
Energumene 80-81
Envoi Allen 81-83
Epatante 36
Faithfulness 83-84
Faugheen 131-132
Faustinovick 36-37
Feel My Pulse 84-85
Financier 85-87
Footpad 144-145
Fox Norton 156-157
Gallahers Cross 37-38
Global Citizen 102-103
Good Man Pat 105
Gosheven 38-39
Heatstroke 39
Heroesandvillains 106
Hitman Fred 106
Hunters Call 57-58
Ifandabut 59-60
Indian Hawk 100
Interconnected 87-88
Jarveys Plate 113
Just Minded 60
Kapcorse 15-16
Killultagh Vic 154

King Roland 40-41, 88-89
Kings Monarch 105
King's Socks 16-17
Kupatana 100
Laurina 130-131
Lough Derg Spirit 41-42
Madison To Monroe 106
Magic Saint 42
Maire Banrigh 105
Master Blueyes 61
Master Tommytucker 43-44
Melon 126-128
Mengli Khan 114-115, 135
Mick Jazz 134-135
Might Bite 140-142
Min 131
Minella Rocco 157
Mister Whitaker 17-18
Monalee 154
Monbeg Zena 106
Moonshine Bay 106
Mr Lingo 106
Ms Parfois 19-20, 157
My Tent Or Yours 133
Native River 137-140
Nebuchadnezzar 44
Net De Treve 105
Never Adapt 45
No Comment 62-63
Off You Go 63-64
On A Promise 45-46
On The Blind Side 21-22, 99-100
Palmers Hill 104, 116
Pontresina 105
Posh Trish 102
Presenting Percy 142-144
Quoi De Neuf 89-90
Road To Respect 149
Robin Roe 46-47

Saldier 135
Samcro 125-126
Sam's Adventure 47
Sam's Gunner 23-24
Santini 99, 117-118
Sebastopol 48-49
Sending Love 106
Shadow Rider 90-91
Shattered Love 147-148
Silver Forever 49
Sizing John 145-146
Slate House 104
Soldier At War 92
Some Man 102
Stay Humble 106
Storm Control 105, 119
Storm Home 105
Style De Vole 50
Summerville Boy 128-129
Supasundae 131, 132
Surf Walk 50-51
Tedham 51
Terrefort 153-154
That's Life 64-65
Thatsy 93-94
The Big Galloper 51-52
The Great Getaway 65
The Hollow Chap 94-95
Thedellercheckout 102
Thistlecrack 149-150
Time To Move On 120-121
Tippingituptonancy 95-96
Topofthegame 52-53
Turning Gold 66
Umndeni 53
Waiting Patiently 152-153
We Have A Dream 132-133
Wilhelm Vonvenster 121-122
Young Bull 97-98